# ALL QUIET ON THE WESTERN FRONT

*Literary Analysis and Cultural Context*

# TWAYNE'S MASTERWORK STUDIES

*Robert Lecker, General Editor*

# ALL QUIET ON THE WESTERN FRONT

*Literary Analysis and Cultural Context*

Richard Arthur Firda

TWAYNE PUBLISHERS • NEW YORK
*Maxwell Macmillan Canada • Toronto*
*Maxwell Macmillan International • New York Oxford Singapore Sydney*

*Twayne's Masterwork Studies No. 129*

*All Quiet on the Western Front: Literary Analysis and Cultural Context*
Richard Arthur Firda

Copyright © 1993 by Twayne Publishers
All rights reserved. No part of this book may be reproduced or transmitted in any
form or by any means, electronic or mechanical, including photocopying, recording, or
by any information storage and retrieval system, without permission in writing from
the Publisher.

Twayne Publishers                    Maxwell Macmillan Canada, Inc.
Macmillan Publishing Company         1200 Eglinton Avenue East
866 Third Avenue                     Suite 200
New York, New York 10022             Don Mills, Ontario M3C 3N1

**Library of Congress Cataloging-in-Publication Data**

Firda, Richard Arthur, 1931–
   All quiet on the western front: literary analysis and cultural
context / Richard Arthur Firda.
      p.   cm. — (Twayne's masterworks series; 129)
   Includes bibliographical references and index.
   ISBN 0-8057-8386-5          ISBN 0-8057-8387-3 (pbk.)
   1. Remarque, Erich Maria, 1898-1970. Im Westen nichts Neues.
   2. World War, 1914–1918—Literature and the war. I. Title.
   II. Series: Twayne's masterworks studies; no. 129.
PT2635.E68I67  1993                                        93-3872
833'.912—dc20                                              CIP

The paper used in this publication meets the minimum requirements of American
National Standard for Information Sciences—Permanence of Paper for Printed Library
Materials. ANSI Z3948–1984. ∞ ™

10 9 8 7 6 5 4 3 2 1 (hc)
10 9 8 7 6 5 4 3 2 1 (pb)

Printed in the United States of America

*For David O'Connell*
*Georgia State University*
*Teacher, Editor, Mentor*

# Contents

Erich Maria Remarque
©*Jerry Bauer*

# Note on the References
# and Acknowledgments

This book assumes that a reader will choose to read an English-language translation of Remarque's novel *All Quiet on the Western Front*. The edition from which I make my references (*AQ*, followed by the page number) is the hardcover text published by Little, Brown in 1975. Available in most libraries, it is notable because it restores material censored in the first American edition of 1929. A Fawcett Crest paperback of *All Quiet*, however, can readily be found at bookstores. Other novels by Remarque especially cited in my book are *The Road Back* (1931) and *Three Comrades* (1937). *Dream Room* (1920) is available only in German; a copy can be located at the Harvard College Library.

I am grateful to all previous and current commentators on Remarque's life and works, especially Christine R. Barker and R. W. Last. I am likewise grateful for having been permitted to read some unpublished correspondence on *All Quiet*. This information, found during a research trip some years ago to Little, Brown, Boston, is referred to in my text. There is as yet no standard literary biography on Remarque's novels, literary career, or film adaptations. Such a book is much more likely to be written now that a Remarque archives has been founded at the University of Osnabrück in Germany. Remarque's widow, the American actress Paulette Goddard, deposited her husband's papers at New York University before her death in April 1990. My own collection of essays in this modest text attempt to give a working background on Remarque before he wrote *All Quiet*: the autobiographical elements in that novel; his style and characterizations; the two novels that are properly called sequels to the themes and problems first introduced in *All Quiet*. Finally, in an effort to show the historical and artistic importance of *All Quiet*, I discuss the American film adaptation and show how the novel compares and contrasts with other equally popular German war fiction in the exciting years of the Weimar Republic.

My sincere thanks to my department chairman, Dr. David O'Connell, for continual encouragement while I was writing this book.

# Chronology: Erich Maria Remarque's Life and Works

1898      Born 22 June in Osnabrück, Germany, of French ancestry. Son of a book printer, Peter Franz Remark, and Anna Maria Stallknecht.

1904      Attends the *Domschule*, a Catholic primary school.

1908–1912      Attends the *Johannisschule*, another Catholic primary school, until he enters the *Katholische Präparande* to prepare academically for admission to the Catholic Teachers' Seminar.

1915–16      Studies at the teachers' seminar. Makes friends in the Traumbude Circle and receives mentor guidance from Fritz Hörstemeier. Comes under the influence of classical music and German romantic poetry and literature.

1916      Drafted into the army, along with other classmates from the teachers' seminar, in November. Undergoes basic training at the Caprivi Barracks in the Osnabrück suburbs and later in the town of Celle.

1917      Sent to the western front in June. Assigned to a duty location behind the Arras front on 14 June. Assigned to a sapper unit on 26 June. Major British offensive in Flanders in June and July. Remarque wounded at Geite-Sankt-Josef. Transferred in August to St. Vincenz Hospital in Duisburg, Germany. Mother dies in September.

1918      Fritz Hörstemeier dies 6 March. Remarque publishes miscellaneous sentimental poetry in the avant-garde journal *Die Schönheit*. Released in October from St. Vincenz and transferred to reserve unit in Osnabrück. Declared fit for return to active duty on 7 November. World War I ends 11 November. Remarque discharged from active army duties. Social and political disorder reigns throughout Germany.

| | |
|---|---|
| 1919 | Plans to resume teacher training studies at the interrupted teachers' seminar. Conflict between teachers and returning students over academic requirements and certificate examinations. Continues with short story and poetry efforts in *Die Schönheit*. Passes elementary teacher's examination on 25 June. Hired as a substitute teacher in Lohne, north of Osnabrück. Contributes music and art criticism to Osnabrück newspapers. Some articles and reviews are signed "Remark." |
| 1920 | Publishes first novel *Die Traumbude* (Dream Room), a thinly disguised account of the Traumbude Circle. Autobiographical, and clearly an amateur's effort, the book would later be disowned by Remarque. On 4 May takes a replacement teaching job in Klein-Berssen; resists the controlling efforts of the local village priest; leaves the position and tries teaching for the third and final time in Nahne, near Osnabrück. |
| 1922 | Drifts about in Osnabrück at sundry jobs; joins the ranks of the Weimar semiemployed. Works as a salesman and a store engraver; also plays the organ at a hospital. Moves to Hannover for his first major postwar position: editor and publicity director for the Continental Rubber Company. Finds his fictional writing style as he writes and edits advertising copy. |
| 1925 | Makes important professional move to Berlin, the publishing capital of Germany. Appointed the picture editor of the newspaper *Sport im Bild*, a publication of the Scherl Verlag that is aimed at the specialized readership of car owners and racing drivers. (Publisher of *Bild* is Alfred Hugenberg, a conservative, nationalist sympathizer.) Marries Jutta Ilse Zambona in Berlin on 14 October. |
| 1927–1928 | Remarque's "racing car novel," *Station am Horizont* (Station on the Horizon), is published serially in *Sport im Bild*. (He will later rework the subject and topic of this popular romance for literature and film.) Begins *Im Westen nichts Neues* (All Quiet on the Western Front). |
| 1928 | *All Quiet* makes the rounds of prestigious German publishers in the early months. Rejected by Fisher Verlag, but accepted by Ullstein with proviso that it be first published in the firm's newspaper, *Die Vossische Zeitung*; serialized 10 November to 9 December. |
| 1929 | Cloth edition of *All Quiet* published on 31 January. Remarque becomes controversial to the Right, disappointing to the Left, and famous with the mass reading public. Despite translations and worldwide celebrity, accepts his fame and wealth modest- |

|      | ly. Henceforth he adopts "Remarque" as a spelling for his last name. |
|------|---------------------------------------------------------------------|
| 1930 | Divorces Jutta Ilsa Zambona on 4 January. Under pressure to write a sequel to *All Quiet*, writes *Der Weg zurück* (The Road Back), based on his return from the war front to civilian life in peacetime Osnabrück. Film premiere in December of *All Quiet* causes protests in Germany. |
| 1931 | *The Road Back* is published in Germany. Buys a villa in the tourist haven Lago Maggiore in Ticino Porto Ronco, Switzerland. Is increasingly charged with betrayal, and censored, by the German military and Nazi party. |
| 1933 | Nazis take over the German government in January. At the end of January Remarque, accompanied by his ex-wife, goes into exile in Switzerland, though he retains his German citizenship. *All Quiet* and *Road* are burned on 10 May by Nazi students in front of Berlin University. Becomes persona non grata. |
| 1937 | *Drei Kameraden* (Three Comrades) is published in English. |
| 1938 | Remarries Jutta Ilse Zambona. Expatriated by Nazis on 4 July; no longer a citizen of Germany. |
| 1939 | Arrives on 23 March in New York, beginning second phase of literary-political exile. Goes to Los Angeles. Wife is denied entry into United States in October and goes to Mexico. |
| 1941 | Becomes legal resident of the United States. *Liebe deinen Nächsten* (Flotsam), the first of three novels portraying lives of exiles, is published abroad in German. |
| 1942 | Moves from Los Angeles to New York City. |
| 1943 | Paintings and art exhibited at Knoedler Galleries in New York in the fall; identified as a connoisseur of French impressionist artwork. Remarque's sister, Elfriede Remark Scholz, executed by Nazis on 16 December. |
| 1946 | *Arc de Triomphe* (Arch of Triumph) published in English and in German; set in prewar Paris, the book is a best-seller. |
| 1947 | Becomes a naturalized U.S. citizen in August. |
| 1948 | Returns to Switzerland, to live there and in the United States. |
| 1952 | His Nazi concentration camp novel *Der Funke Leben* (Spark of Life) is published in German. Criticized by readers and critics, who also challenge its authenticity. |
| 1954 | Father dies in Bad Rothenfelde (Osnabrück area). *Zeit zu leben und Zeit zu sterben* (A Time to Love and a Time to Die) is pub- |

lished in German and in English. This World War II novel replicates themes and characterizations found in *All Quiet*.

1955    *The Last Act*, G. W. Pabst's feature film about Hitler's last days for which Remarque wrote the scenario, is premiered in Berlin in August. Film is shown in August at the Edinburgh Film Festival.

1956    *Der schwarze Obelisk* (*The Black Obelisk*) marked by a return to the autobiographical source material of Remarque's life in Osnabrück in the 1920s, is published in German. His play *Die letzte Station* (The Last Station; later translated into English as "Full Circle" [1973]) premieres in Berlin in September.

1957    Living in Hollywood, writes and advises on Universal Studios' adaptation of *A Time to Love and a Time to Die*. In May divorces Jutta in Mexico.

1958    Marries the American film actress Paulette Goddard in February.

1961    *Der Himmel kennt keine Günstlinge* (Heaven Has No Favorites), a racing car novel and romance that reworks themes and episodes from Remarque's days as a newspaper editor, is published in English and in German.

1962    Publishes *Die Nacht von Lissabon* (The Night in Lisbon).

1964    Awarded on 1 November the Justus Möser Medal from the city of Osnabrück for distinguished and honored service.

1967    Recognized and honored by the West German government with *Das Grosse Verdienstkreuz* (Distinguished Service Cross of the Order of Merit).

1968    Recognized by his literary peers in West Germany by election to membership in the Deutsche Akademie für Sprache und Dichtung (German Academy for Language and Literature).

1970    Dies on 25 September in Saint Agnes Hospital in Locarno, Switzerland.

1971    *Schatten im Paradies* (Shadows in Paradise), a novel that depicts the lives of German exiles in New York City during World War II, is published posthumously.

1979    A feature film remake of *All Quiet* is shown on U.S. television on 14 November.

# LITERARY AND HISTORICAL CONTEXT

# 1

# A Citizen of the German Empire

The German writer Erich Maria Remarque was born during the second Wilhelmine empire on 22 June 1898 in the northern Protestant city of Osnabrück, which now lies in the German state of Lower Saxony.[1] Remarque, born Erich Paul Remark, was the son of a Catholic book printer and binder, Peter Franz Remark, and Anna Maria Stallknecht. His parents were poor and came from a line of craftsmen. Remarque was proud of his humble Franco-German background and would later change the spelling of his name from the German back to the original French version.

The writer's full and active life was destined to span a wide range of political, social, and historical changes that affected not only Germany but Europe and the United States. These changes were incubated in the German empire under the blundering hand of Wilhelm II, who was both king of Prussia and emperor (*kaiser*) of Germany. Wilhelm II was the last representative of the Hohenzollern monarchy, and he was responsible, soon after his accession to the throne in 1890, for dismissing Otto Bismarck as German chancellor. Remarque also witnessed the outbreak of World War I in August 1914. Yugoslavian nationalists had initiated the immediate conflict, and

Austria soon implored Germany to support the cause of Austrian justice. Germany, however, with its own pretensions to European leadership and economic hegemony, entered the conflict for mostly nationalistic reasons, not just to defend Austria against the threat of Serbian political assassins. As a young student, Remarque was drafted into the German army in 1916 and endured the spectacle of his country's defeat in November 1918.

The German Reichstag, including the quarreling Social Democrats, listened to the emperor's petition for political cooperation among the many factions of conservatives, centrists, leftists, and Social Democrats. Most German politicians supported the idea of the war, and its execution, at the beginning. However, Germany's eventual surrender and the harrowing armistice negotiations with the Allies were both humiliating and difficult for the German nation. Germans agreed only reluctantly to the formation of the Weimar Republic, whose "birth" on 9 November 1918 was truly an accident of political history, a matter of socialist timing from the balcony of the Reichstag over purported takeover plans by leftist politicians who were dreaming of a central government based on Soviet precedent.

The hollow, sometimes vague phraseology of the Weimar constitution, written in 1919 in Weimar, the hallowed city of Goethe and Schiller, was tolerated by the German populace as a desperate attempt to restore social and political order to a country being torn apart by dissension and guilt over the recent military fiasco. Left-wing socialists (the Sparticists) wanted to remake the country according to the Soviet model. The Right still questioned the validity of Germany's (and Austria's) terms of settlement under the Allies. The French and Belgians were vindictively demanding excessive economic reparations. The victors proposed that Allied armies occupy German land west of the Rhine. Some territory of the former German empire was lost permanently, representing a significant shrinkage of governmental control. Since German capitalists continued to spread the notion that socialists would betray the country to leftist rule, the early political days of the Weimar Republic were far from settled. Remarque worked in his hometown, Osnabrück, at this time as a salesman, wrote occasional poetry, and worked on the local newspaper, trying to survive.

# A Citizen of the German Empire

At the end of the Great War, Remarque joined the lines of returning, alienated German veterans who were trying to find the "road back" into civilian life. He drifted reluctantly back into the provincial backwater of Osnabrück, a beautiful and ancient place whose claims to historical and cultural importance lay in its ties to the Hanseatic League formally organized by German merchants in 1358. The peace treaty of the Thirty Years' War had been announced from the steps of the Osnabrück town hall on 25 October 1648. Remarque worked as an elementary school teacher (*Volksschullehrer*) from 1 August 1919 to 20 November 1920. This profoundly unhappy experience was documented under the guise of fiction in Remarque's second major novel, *The Road Back* (1931). Remarque could never submit to the unbearable isolation and numbing routine of the grade schools, and to the thumb of the conservative teaching regime. He drifted next, in the fall of 1922, to Hannover, a prominent northern German capital and industrial city with English connections, where he worked as an advertising editor for the *Echo Continental*, the house organ of the Continental Rubber Company. Continental's main business was to sell tires and indirectly support the fledgling automobile industry by promoting tourism. Remarque cut his professional writing teeth at Continental using the hard, pointed language of business and commercial German. This job was decidedly several steps higher than teaching on the German scale of professional and social advancement, but the real drawing card for Remarque was the lure of a future position in Berlin, which was becoming the true center of Weimar life and culture.

The Weimar political style, ostensibly liberal and socialist, would be a melancholy and short-lived dream; its collapse was followed by Hitler's takeover in January 1933. But in 1925 the Republic's golden era had not yet been written off. Figures such as Bertolt Brecht (theater), Wassily Kandinsky (art), Fritz Lang and F. W. Murnau (film), and Marlene Dietrich dominated the Weimar cultural landscape, displaying the originality and artistic leadership that have forever defined the dazzling display of Weimar talent. Peter Gay, whose book *Weimar Culture: The Outsider as Insider* (1968) remains an outstanding English-language account of Weimar cultural glory, provides a broad picture of the political and cultural contradictions and the special background against which Remarque's achievement as a new novelist must be measured.[2]

Remarque arrived in Berlin in 1925 to work at Scherl Verlag, a bastion of journalism headed by the politically conservative Alfred Hugenberg. Hugenberg's chief competition in Berlin publishing was the Ullstein conglomerate, a family enterprise and in many ways a successful example of liberal German Jewish capitalism; it would provide the setting for Remarque's antiwar novel *Im Westen nichts Neues* (All Quiet on the Western Front).[3] Hitler and the Nazis would never forget that *All Quiet* was originally published by the "House of Ullstein," a symbol of Weimar liberalism, an establishment that had long been open to pacifist authors and other writers of many persuasions. *All Quiet* was burned early on in the Nazi takeover of power.

When Remarque published *All Quiet* in 1929, his was not the only war novel being written. Specifically European war novels assessing the World War I military experience included Henri Barbusse's *Le Feu* (Under Fire, 1918) and Roland Dorgelès's *Les Croix de bois* (Wooden Crosses, 1920). The postwar American point of view was variously presented by two established novelists, Willa Cather (*One of Ours*, 1923) and John Dos Passos (*Three Soldiers*, 1922). In Germany, Arnold Zweig's *Der Streit um den Sergeanten Grischa* (The Case of Sergeant Grischa, 1928) and Ludwig Renn's *Krieg* (War, 1929) competed in sales and in popularity with the reading public. Zweig's book, a fictionalized account of the fate of a Russian prisoner of war, was favored by the German Left as a satirical criticism of the "war machine," while Renn's book was deemed objective to a fault, assigning neither blame nor praise to the German soldiers. Although neither officers nor enlisted men express any direct criticism of the war in *War*, there are plenty of direct references to fighting. In contrast to Zweig and Renn, with whose works Remarque must have been familiar, *All Quiet* fulfills Remarque's own standard for the ideal war novel: it should convey the lesson of comradeship at the front, that is, the experience of war ought to say something about the bonding of men through the terrible exigencies of war; and expression of the war experience should be impressionistic, a series of episodes colored by the feelings of the enlisted men themselves, however simple or elemental.

# A Citizen of the German Empire

By 1929, a good ten years after the war, enough time had passed for some Germans to have either forgotten the war or to have confronted the fact of the German military defeat. German business and the German army, however, had never accepted that defeat, and both groups, as powerful as ever, enlisted emotional support for their cause from the middle class. Civilian survivors like Remarque, however, were still oppressed by memories of life at the front. Remarque would claim that his memories were a catalyst for writing *All Quiet*.[4] He was also politically alienated, a pacifist, and a novice in Berlin's artistic circles. Remarque was not then, nor would he ever be, identified with the platform of any political party. When the map of Europe began to change ominously in the 1930s, Remarque chose the way of nonalignment: he went into exile around January 1933, moving to his villa in the Italian part of Switzerland, a neutral country. After leaving Germany both spiritually and physically, he would observe German culture and politics from afar. *All Quiet*, however, was his first step in dissociating himself from German political life.

*All Quiet* became an artistic and commercial success not only in Germany but also in England, France, and the United States.[5] Some German intellectuals resented the idea of a best-selling author in their midst; the concept was very foreign to traditional notions of German artistic achievement. Remarque was regarded by the Weimar German Left as indecisive and noncommittal. His natural allies accused him of not having gone far enough in his criticism of the war. And why did he "accept" the protest of the Nazi Joseph Goebbels against the American film adaptation of *All Quiet* when it opened at a Berlin movie theater on 6 December 1930?

After fleeing to Switzerland and then coming to live in the United States in 1939 as a wealthy exile under the protection of the American government, Remarque wrote four other landmark novels: *Arc de Triomphe* (Arch of Triumph, 1946), *Der schwarze Obelisk* (The Black Obelisk, 1957), *Die Nacht von Lissabon* (The Night in Lisbon, 1964), and *Schatten im Paradies* (Shadows in Paradise, 1972). The last of these books was published posthumously and is a veiled account of Remarque's life as an exile-observer of the Germans among the New York German exile community during the Second World War.

Many of Remarque's novels were made into Hollywood feature films, and his contacts with the Hollywood community remained strong throughout his life.[6] Film producers and directors appreciated the accessibility of his novels and their episodic structure. They were easily converted into popular film works of art and cinematic romance.

Though none of these four novels replicate the content of *All Quiet* or the resonance it achieved with his first reading audience, they are all rooted, like *All Quiet*, in Remarque's own life, both as a German and as an exile. These novels reflect the role Remarque came to prefer of being an artist-observer of key cultural and political events of the twentieth century. In his later years, however, living in splendid isolation in Switzerland after years of exile in America, Remarque seemed to fulfill the prophecy in those precipitating factors that had led to the writing of *All Quiet*: cultural alienation.

He had survived Weimar, Hitler, World War II, and the postwar recovery of Germany. He had become an American citizen in 1957. Remarque's whole life, it seemed to him, had been a vital part of German and European cultural and historical change, a meditative witness more philosophical than political. His books had also given art a broad voice in the marketplace. At the time of his death in Switzerland in September 1970, Remarque was labeled by both the American and European press as the "Last of the Lost Generation," a reference, perhaps, to his role as a sensitive, unhappy witness to, and judge of, the precipitous confluence of history, politics, culture, and art in the twentieth century.

# 2

# The Importance of the Work

From 1929 to 1975, 3,425,000 hardcover and paperback copies of *All Quiet* were sold (latest figures available). Although these numbers are out of date, *All Quiet* remains in print and is read by readers all over the world.[1] For the English-language reader at least, the relevance of Remarque's novel is still found in those humanistic and artistic qualities that made it a popular success among Germans in the 1920s. Then as now, readers responded to its criticism of war as a destroyer of civilized values, to its assertion that war is often fought for reasons that have little to do with improving men morally or ethically.

The first readers of *All Quiet* were also attracted to Remarque's effective study of Paul Bäumer, a common German soldier, not one of the favored officers, who in Germany typically inherited their special military status. Paul Bäumer is a young man with whom most readers can identify naturally and sympathetically. Bäumer's impressionistic experience of war as a prelude to dying is also a tragic event that reflects many readers' concept of the anonymity of war, which is tantamount to an early meeting with the Great Reaper. Through what the reader learns about Bäumer's youth, his interrupted education, and the poignant suffering of his family, however, his death on the western

front is not anonymous. The reader can even accept some of the jingoistic reasons he enlisted in the army. Anyone who has bent (unwilling-
ly) to a higher authority will relate to the deterministic structure of the
German social and political system from which Bäumer comes. His
spiritual problems are both individual and general. The human and
national dilemma of war is accessible to people everywhere.

Bäumer's brief service on the western front gives the careful
observer a momentary insight into the universal war experience; especially valuable for the average reader, this insight verifies and even
articulates the suspicion, however private, that in war everything rests
on the needless sacrifice of the common soldier. Bäumer becomes such
a soldier. He symbolizes a passive, sensitive, and meditative heroism.
Like all antiwar novels, *All Quiet* presents the rather startling image of
the foot soldier as the antihero, the antithesis in this instance of
German heroic rhetoric. In 1919 the former German storm trooper
officer Ernst Jünger published a record of his own experiences on the
front, *In Stahlgewittern* (The Storm of Steel).[2] War for Jünger's officer
is a patriotic, liberating experience, unlike the experience of Remarque's
disillusioned antihero. Jünger became an exponent of war as the arena
for defending classic nationalist principles. A mystic, he argued that
war gives men, especially German combatants, a sense of life's savage
and visionary heart. Remarque, on the other hand, chose to debunk
both the "beauty" of war and military heroism as romantic, deceptive
experiences. Before his death, Bäumer fears that neither the generation
preceding his nor the one to follow would understand his own generation. These thoughts were heretical and denied the possibility of heroism. If the nation required unselfish heroism, the traditional sacrifice,
to preserve the continuity of its people, *All Quiet* works clearly against
such a facile concept of military heroism.

With its antiwar voice, *All Quiet* claimed to speak for a distinct
generation of alienated Germans—those veterans of the war who real-
ized that the personal cost of the Great War was a loss of cultural values. These ex-combatants were neither defenders of the lost war nor
idealists or closet revolutionaries. Remarque's foreword to *All Quiet*
reflects this neutralist stance. He suggests that war be judged by standards that avoid political extremes: "This book," Remarque notes, "is

to be neither an accusation nor a confession, and least of all an adventure." Remarque was pleading a different case in 1929 than he would advocate later; his position also avoided the idealistic view of war, so fond to the traditional German militaristic mentality, namely, that war is an act of rejuvenation and rebirth, a Nietzschean opportunity for soldier and officer to become harbingers of historical and social change.

In his early novel *The Way of Sacrifice* (1928) the idealistic Fritz von Unruh argues that war has truly healed contradictory forces in the German social and political fabric.[3] Remarque's antihero, however, rejects the forces that defined the ruling German ethos: school, army, and a deterministic economic system that maintained distinctions between the rich and poor. This rejection occurs after Paul Bäumer probes his sensibility and feelings. Life itself emerges as the most desirable value of all. Remarque was actually redefining the man of the future in true humanistic fashion, seeing the common man as an independent agent operating above mass social and political norms. German militarists and political conservatives, by contrast, had confused conformity and patriotic duty with character and individuality. *All Quiet* says that ultimately there is no higher cause than to serve the survival of life. War works against the will of the living to survive. Remarque's book was among the first in Germany to challenge the common assumption that Germany's leading capitalists and politicians stood united against the enemy; they had, in fact, a vested interest in prolonging, not ending, the conflict.

– Both the theme and central character of *All Quiet* reinforce the reader's suspicion that most World War I combatants served and suffered for reasons they scarcely understood. Through the eyes and vision of that central character we watch his understanding grow; eventually he learns that the promise of a peaceful life in a stable nation is broken by war. The reader becomes aware that war exposes all men, wherever they are fighting, to the same painful dilemma. As they fight, men lose not only their civility but their ethics. In this sense, *All Quiet* remains a quintessential pacifist work.

# 3

# Reception in the Marketplace

The critical reception of Remarque's first major novel in Germany was polarized and often marked by the political and cultural bias conferred by a critic's social or economic status. These political and social factors inhibited a fair critical assessment of the book. German critics and readers have often addressed only the novel's political issues, ignoring its aesthetic and literary aspects.

Upon publication, *All Quiet* became a world best-seller, a unique publishing event—close to a million copies were sold. Even by 1977, however, the novel's best-seller status remained a problem. In an article published in *Modern Language Review*, A. F. Bance asked, how can a book that has sold so many copies warrant serious critical attention? (359). Bance charged that Remarque and his German publisher, Ullstein, had conspired to initiate a well-managed sales campaign. Remarque did in fact withdraw from the German public and was thus sought out for interviews. He became controversial, a literary cause célèbre hounded by readers and political factions alike. Ullstein issued an extensively documented publicity brochure that gave sales figures for both Germany and abroad and, under categories like "truth," "pacifism," "heroism," and "antipatriotism," quoted letters from German notables and from newspapers around the country. *Der*

## Reception in the Marketplace

*Kampf um Remarque* (the battle around Remarque), according to Ullstein, was the hottest issue in Germany. It is a matter of record that Ullstein instigated this "battle," which served its commercial interests.[1]

Many Germans, even some who had not actually read the novel, had an opinion about Remarque's realistic portrayal of war, which purportedly underlay the genuinely effective style and plangent tone of the text. *All Quiet* became a crossover book—it successfully skipped over the traditional boundary line (which, of course, exists to this day) between popular and serious fiction. In the 1920s Remarque's novel was not only bought but read. His unadorned language struck a nerve among the German working class and rendered familiar a complex experience (war and suffering) that had been shared by both the upper and lower classes. *All Quiet*'s skillful avoidance of dreary documentation and focus instead on Paul Bäumer's singular destiny as an unwitting victim of the Great War created a moving spiritual text that impressed the German reading masses. Here was an "artist" who succeeded in communicating with the average reader.

Though *All Quiet* was translated into 25 languages—a not insignificant record for a twentieth-century German novel—pertinent factors preceding its publication might serve to explain the confluence of its publication and its wide readership; these events can also serve to either clarify or obstruct a reader's understanding and appreciation of the novel. With a novel as politically sensitive as *All Quiet*, it is especially important to uncover any differences between the author's professed aesthetic and personal goals and his underlying professional motives. Remarque, for example, claimed that his only reason for writing *All Quiet* was to escape his depression and despair, the lasting, spiritual crisis, induced by his service in the Great War. Catharsis, he said, not financial gain, was his ostensible goal in writing a book that would be a novelty for many Germans: a pacifist's plea for an end to war and a rejection of the idea of war as purification of the national psyche.[2] One can speculate, however, whether Remarque intentionally wrote a war novel very different from what many Germans expected to read.

Since its author was opposed to the corruption and misuse of men by war, *All Quiet*'s only hope of publication lay in being sponsored by a publisher strong enough to survive all accusations of public betrayal, especially charges from the Right. As Peter de Mendelssohn reports, a natural first choice for Remarque was the prestigious S. Fisher Verlag, the publisher of classic German literature, including the canonic trio of Thomas Mann, Hugo von Hofmannsthal, and Rainer Maria Rilke.[3] Fisher was not receptive, however, and rejected *All Quiet* on the grounds that it was a new novel by an unknown author, thus casting doubt on Remarque's ability ever to attain the cachet of an established author. Fisher's logo symbolized acceptance and achievement within the intellectual community, a boon that Fisher refused to grant Remarque. Remarque went elsewhere with his novel, and *All Quiet* was finally accepted, conditionally, by Ullstein, a liberal house and a publishing giant.[4] Remarque never forgot the frenetic conditions of getting published in Weimar Berlin, and he would always exact in later years the most favorable financial and publishing conditions for his works.

Remarque agreed to forgo cloth publication until *All Quiet* had first been serialized in Ullstein's "old" newspaper, the beloved *Vossische Zeitung*, a favorite of Berlin's intellectuals. Prepublication of novels in a newspaper was common, and Remarque's novel was printed in the "Voss" from 10 November to 9 December 1928. The novel passed muster with the Berlin literary establishment, though as subsequent events would bear out, the literary and critical assessment of Remarque in the pages of the Voss reflected how limited the readership of that newspaper actually was. Not all Germans were political centrists or liberals. The critical comment in the Voss was simply the first volley—shot in Remarque's favor—in the ensuing controversy. Other early supportive reviews of *All Quiet* were written by the noted German expressionist playwright Ernst Toller and the Austrian dramatist Carl Zuckmayer, who, in a stunning review for the *Berliner Illustrierte*, noted that the book would draw all humanity together over the sad fate of the postwar generation.[5] Toller's and Zuckmayer's fair and unprejudiced criticisms, in the best tradition of German centrism, were reasoned considerations of not only the book's claim to speak for Germany's "lost generation" of 1914–18 but also of its pacifist agenda.

## Reception in the Marketplace

Remarque received more negative, politically inspired criticism from, surprisingly, both the Right and the Left. Each side of the political spectrum had its own reasons for rejecting Remarque's book and his apparent decision to rest his case against the Great War on Paul Bäumer's war experience. The attack of German ultranationalists on *All Quiet* and its author focused on the novel's implicit indictment of capitalists, politicians, and the German military. These right-wingers retaliated by claiming that Remarque was a Jew, that his real name was "Krämer" (shopkeeper), which, as every German knew, was the authentic (though revised) spelling of "Remark," the author's first family name on German soil, as opposed to "Remarque," which spelling appears in the records on Remarque's French-based ancestors.[6] The unproven charge of Remarque's Jewish background was doubtless spread in the pages of Hitler's National Socialist newspaper, the *Völkischer Beobachter*, which reviewed *All Quiet* in June 1929. Many Germans read this review, as well as a number of books specifically written as ad hominem arguments against Remarque. The most popular of these satirical texts, *Hat Remarque wirklich gelebt* (Did Remarque Really Live?), was written in 1929 by "Mynona" ("anonymous," from the German form of the word spelled backwards).[7] Mynona, in turn, was the pseudonym of the German writer Dr. Salomo Friedländer. Friedländer tried to expose Remarque as a fraud and a literary imposter. He was especially critical of Remarque's military service.

By contrast, the German Left saw Remarque's neutrality—his pacifism—as a betrayal of his antiwar stance and hence obligation not only to speak out directly against war but to oppose the war experience actively and openly. The German Left was clearly dissatisfied with Remarque's apolitical stand, his refusal to point an accusing finger at the united front of the German governing class. As a leftist spokesman and novelist, the critic Arnold Zweig felt compelled to show that Remarque's silence was humiliating to progressive political forces, that Remarque had failed to ask the most important question, the one about the social and economic origins of the First World War.[8] For German communists and socialists, *All Quiet* was palpably barren of revolutionary sentiment. Remarque would never climb the proverbial barricades against capitalism. This particular criticism of the novel and its author lingered on into 1932, when Carl von Ossietzky, a political newspaper commentator, made the point that Remarque had let slip a grand opportunity to speak out on a theme that "divides Germany into camps: the theme of war."[9] Ossietzky meant, of course, that Remarque had spoken out but failed to follow up with a reformist's political program. In May 1933 Goebbels and the German Students' League summarily ended the arguments aroused by *All Quiet* by throwing the novel into a fire. Writings of Sigmund Freud, Emil Ludwig, Karl Marx, and Heinrich Mann (the brother of Thomas Mann) were all banned and burned at the same time.

In England and America, however, the critical reception and publishing history of *All Quiet* took a different direction. By 1929 English writers and veterans had begun to tackle the World War I novel, and British publication of *All Quiet* would precede American publication of the novel. *All Quiet*'s American publication was at least partly inspired, according to the record, by the prospect of achieving best-seller status. Both British and American publication, however, were guided finally by financial considerations, which were vigorously pursued by Remarque's agent, Otto Klement. Financial success had forced Remarque into the dubious position of continually having to demand favorable conditions of publication.

In England the noted critic and writer Herbert Read wrote outstanding and supportive essays on *All Quiet* for the *Manchester Guardian Weekly* and the *National and Athenaeum*, both journals with a selective readership. "German War Books," the *Guardian* piece, placed Remarque's novel in the company of previous German texts on the subject by Fritz von Unruh, Ernst Toller, and Arnold Zweig and did not hesitate to call *All Quiet* "the greatest of all war books" for the immediacy of the war experience conveyed in its pages. Read noted that the book was neither pacifist propaganda nor specifically German, but rather a book of the common soldier, as truthful about one side as about the other.[10] In the *Athenaeum* book review, Read directed his commentary toward Paul Bäumer's symbolic role as a spokesman for a "lost generation"; the British critic agreed that the "war's only good gift" was a mutual respect gained by each side for the other's sufferings, as well as a sense of comradeship.[11]

Several months after the British publication of *All Quiet*, Remarque exchanged letters with the noted British general Sir Ian Hamilton, and these were excerpted in 1929 in the pages of the journal *Life and Letters*.[12] Hamilton, a combatant and great military man in World War I, was sent an advance copy of *All Quiet* by its British publisher, G. P. Putnam's. After reading the book, Hamilton said that there was more to war than Remarque's affecting realism—for instance, there is patriotism, and the knowledge that life is more than dying for an unknown cause. Nevertheless, he believed that Remarque had done a splendid job. In reply to Hamilton, Remarque noted that "patriotism is only seemingly absent, because the simple soldier never spoke of it" (Hamilton, 405). For Remarque, patriotism lay in the deed, not in the word; he said that he had restricted himself to portraying the "purely human aspect of war experience" (Hamilton, 407). Despite Hamilton's brief and ambiguous reference to the great and terrible "counter-power" of the romance and beauty of war, he and Remarque resolved their differences amicably in the broad terrain of appreciative understanding. Indeed, Hamilton invited Remarque to write another book.

Unpublished correspondence of 1929 between Putnam's, the British publisher, and Little, Brown in Boston, *All Quiet*'s American publisher, gives the reader interesting insight into the background of American publication [13]. The British firm became an intermediary between Remarque and Little, Brown, but only after difficult and lengthy negotiations. These letters, and the publishing contract that resulted, reveal that Remarque was both courted and protected by Little, Brown as a literary prize. The correspondence also reveals signs that Little, Brown was not above using strategies in printing *All Quiet* that lay on the borderline of sound publishing practice. Little, Brown agreed to censor *All Quiet*, by excising certain passages, after the judges of the Book-of-the-Month Club had voted to make the book its June 1929 selection. The British edition, on the other hand, was published in full. Alfred R. McIntyre, the president of Little, Brown, in a letter printed 24 July 1929 in the *New Republic*, attempted to defend the censorship by pointing out the stringency of Massachusetts law, but he failed to mention his firm's compelling interest in meeting the book club's request for additional excisions. The passages in question—which revolve around latrine and hospital episodes—remained censored until 1975, when Little, Brown published an edition based on the original German text of 1929.

Neither Henry Seidel Canby nor Frank Hill, who wrote laudatory reviews in the *Saturday Review of Literature* and the *New York Herald Tribune*, respectively, mentioned the censored passages.[14] The *New York Times* carried a report on the controversy; this near silence on the censorship issue reveals much about not only the media but the fear of censorship by the legal authorities.[15] Canby and Hill might have been unwilling to review the book under controversial circumstances, but it is incredible that Remarque (and his agent) agreed to the censorship. All parties involved, however, sensed the potential for tremendous sales of *All Quiet* in the United States. Indeed, after a first printing of 100,000 copies, Little, Brown's printing total reached 300,000 copies at the end of the first year, an excellent figure for a new German writer in the competitive American market.

Remarque's status in the United States, as perceived not only by his first publisher but by the Hollywood studios, surely influenced the enduring reputation of his novel among his more educated admirers as well as among his broader reading public. Having become a financial success in the eyes of the Hollywood film community, he was invited by Carl Laemmle, the head of Universal Studios, to agree to a film adaptation, a serious film for a world audience. This film was duly made, by the American director Lewis Milestone, and premiered in the United States on 21 April 1930. Lew Ayres played the role of Paul Bäumer. The film was very popular in the United States but managed to irritate many Germans when it opened in Berlin in December 1930. Goebbels, later notorious as Hitler's propaganda minister, was there with pickets to protest the latest American "insult" to German honor and the German military.[16] Remarque chose, once again, not to intervene in the ensuing debate between conservatives and liberals, a decision for which he was roundly criticized.

## Reception in the Marketplace

Contemporary literary criticism of Remarque centers primarily on *All Quiet*, his novel of the Great War, although his later novels, like *Arch of Triumph* and *Shadows in Paris*, are appreciated for their evocative description of German exiles in Paris and the United States during World War II. Five studies—one in German, another from England, and three from the United States—have attempted an overall survey of Remarque's life and work.[17] Recent literary criticism has also revived interest in Remarque's later life as a literary exile in Switzerland and the United States. *All Quiet* figures prominently in the discussion in Bernard Bergonzi's *Heroes' Twilight* (1966) and Paul Fussell's *The Great War and Modern Memory* (1975) about the enduring fiction that emanated from the First World War.[18] Both Bergonzi and Fussell cite Remarque's novel as a permanent German contribution to twentieth-century European literary and political history. During the cold war and the postwar division of Western and Eastern Europe, Remarque was remembered by socialist and communist critics as an opponent of German militarism and capitalism and assigned a stronger role in this political struggle than was perhaps justified. The former German Democratic Republic, East Germany, was especially active in assimilating Remarque into the canon of German socialist literature. Finally, the efforts of German literary scholars have led to the establishment of an Erich Maria Remarque archive in his birthplace, Osnabrück, where his personal correspondence and literary records are being collected and documented for future generations. In the United States the library of New York University holds primary manuscripts and papers relevant to Remarque's life and career.

# A READING

# 4

# A Writer's Apprenticeship

In a 1929 interview Remarque discussed his earlier struggle to find both a literary style and a voice for writing serious literature.[1] He acknowledged that *All Quiet* was preceded by at least eight years of literary and professional apprenticeship. Remarque discovered that popular German models of literary prose were wrong and inappropriate for him. It was in this sense that his 1929 war novel was a literary breakthrough for more than just the quality of the writing. *All Quiet* also signaled the abandonment of a false standard of aesthetic achievement.

But the reader of *All Quiet* also encounters a realistic style of expression—brief and direct language that makes the novel aesthetically accessible to everyone. Remarque's experience in the practical, everyday world of advertising in Hannover and his subsequent job editing a journal in Berlin rid his language to a remarkable extent of digression and ponderous sentence structures. He abandoned the pomposity and pretension of his youthful literary efforts during this crucial period working in the marketplace of German publishing. In addition, the cities of Osnabrück, Hannover, and Berlin were formative influences and played unique roles in nurturing Remarque's commercial and artistic success as a writer.

Remarque's future success could not have been predicted by his depressing family background. Art and literature were absent from his distinctly lower-class provincial upbringing. Neither of his two sisters showed any interest in writing; his mother was a common, hardworking woman, and his working-class father's primary contact with books was handling them as a bookbinder. As far as can be ascertained, Remarque never attended a *Mittelschule* (high school) or even a *Gymnasium*, which remains to this day in Germany the equivalent of a private school education as well as the normal preparation for university study. Remarque would have received the *Abitur*, a prestigious certificate, had he graduated from a gymnasium; social and professional advancement could have followed quickly. If young Remarque dreamed of escaping a predestined career as a blue-collar worker's apprentice, which his father had been forced to become, he had only two choices: becoming either a Catholic priest or a primary school teacher. The latter course seemed more possible: it required neither financial expenditures nor passing a stringent entrance examination, though the training of public school teachers was subject, in Remarque's day, to the religious denominational oversight of Catholics and Protestants. (The federal government would loosen such religious control in the future.) For whatever reasons, Remarque never considered a career as a Catholic priest. The future author doubtless imagined a freer life as a Volksschullehrer. Formal requirements for a Catholic primary school teacher's certificate were approximately four years of courses, divided between a *Präparande* (preparatory studies) and a Catholic *Schullehrerseminar* (teachers' seminar), taken in sequence. Formal training for public school teachers reflected the influential role of Catholic or Protestant religious/political affiliations under the Berlin-ruled Prussian federal educational and religious authorities. Remarque thus studied at the Catholic teacher training institute in Osnabrück from 1912 to 1916, at which time he interrupted his classes and became an army recruit. He finished the teachers' seminar only after returning to Osnabrück in 1918.

It was in 1915 that Remarque had his first important, sustaining contact with art and literature. He became acquainted with an artistic circle of aspiring Osnabrück writers, painters, and poets. This group, the so-called Traumbude (Dream Room) Circle, was led by an older man and second-rate artist named Fritz Hörstemeier (1882–1918)—all but unknown in the history of German painting—who functioned as a mentor to students like Remarque who had to shift for themselves. Hanns-Gerd Rabe, Remarque's contemporary and his first biographer, has noted Remarque's susceptibility to Hörstemeier's seductive and erroneous concepts of life and art (1970, 208). As a *schwärmender Idealist* (dreaming idealist), Remarque cannot be faulted for succumbing to Hörstemeier's facile and vulgar aesthetic program, which strove toward a single organic definition of "beauty," especially the beauty of the German provincial soul as exhibited in the nobility of its art, music, and poetry. An important understanding of Remarque's artistic development at this time can be gleaned from his rendering of these early experiences in the Hörstemeier circle in his *Künstlerroman* (artistic novel) *Die Traumbude* (Dream Room, 1920).[2] The Künstlerroman, a fictional genre stressing the development of an artist's life, dominated early nineteenth-century German fiction. Goethe, Eduard Mörike, and Gottfried Keller were just a few of the writers who wrote novels in which the central character is an artist. Faced with such a venerable history, it is not surprising that an aspiring novelist like young Remarque should have attempted a Künstlerroman. *Dream Room* is a rarely available, seldom read novel that, compared with its famous models, has little literary merit. But it is invaluable as not only a deeply felt tribute to early twentieth-century Osnabrück but as a revealing study of the secret dreams and hopes of its young author.

A small book adorned by German *Jugendstil* (art nouveau) design, the 213-page *Dream Room* is by "Erich Remark"; Remarque had not yet permanently adopted the original spelling of his ancestral name. Hörstemeier appears as the character Fritz Schramm, a cult figure and elder spokesman. Remarque is Ernst Winter, a student acolyte. Schramm's intimate attic apartment in Osnabrück is a composite of Hörstemeier's and Remarque's living quarters and gives the novel its name. The "dream room" is a magic place for conversations about art, music, and the German culture. Nietzsche's aesthetics has catalyzed the program for cultural renewal of the group that meets in the dream room, where young Winter expresses his feelings about

Frédéric Chopin and Richard Wagner. Some of Schramm's poetry is read, as well as poems by Goethe and Joseph von Eichendorff, a German romantic. The opening pages of *Dream Room* focus on Schramm's movement through the streets of Osnabrück, drawing utensils in hand, surrounded by the springtime scent of lilacs. Schramm postpones his appointment with an elderly woman; he stops instead to draw the view of a garden door. An artist's impulse wins out over banalities like keeping appointments. Here we see young Remarque's penchant for facile romanticism and for promoting the urgency of artistic sensitivity. The novel ends with Ernst Winter abandoning love and a career in the big city. He returns to Osnabrück and to the arms of the unpretentious Elizabeth, who symbolizes stability and permanence in the artist's quest for identity. Schramm dies, and for Winter, new desires require a new vision of life.

Remarque would never again portray his birthplace so fancifully and romantically. In a later novel, *Der schwarze Obelisk* (The Black Obelisk, 1956), though it is also autobiographical and set almost entirely in Osnabrück (under the name Werdenbrück), the central theme concerns not the making of an artist but rather the hero's ingenuity in a time of economic crisis. The setting is Osnabrück in 1923, and Remarque's point of view is that of a cool, detached observer of the events that are forcing cultural and historical change in the city and its citizens. *Obelisk* is the work of a stoic writer who renders life's suffering and deprivation realistically. *Obelisk* is also a roman à clef that alludes to the author's work as a theater critic, at the end of World War I, for the *Osnabrücker Landeszeitung*, a local newspaper. By 1920 Remarque was attending Osnabrück cultural lectures but as a newspaper theater critic he refused to sanction the slender stage productions of the city's overly zealous theatrical groups. As he had done since 1918, when he wrote the poems "The Woman with the Golden Eyes," "I and You," and "Out of My Youth" for the Dresden arts monthly *Die Schönheit* (Beauty), he continued to publish lyric poems and prose sketches (Rabe 1970, 208). (*Die Schönheit* would publish *Dream Room*, the remaining copies of which Ullstein reportedly bought up in an attempt to sell *All Quiet*, and its author, as a literary "discovery.")

## A Writer's Apprenticeship

Not content to suffer the limitations of Osnabrück's cultural life, Remarque left in October 1922 for greener pastures in the neighboring city of Hannover. He found a job there that would improve his social and professional status: a position as an editor and advertising manager for the *Echo Continental*, a trade magazine for customers of the Continental Rubber Company. The work and the daily routine at the urban offices of the *Echo Continental* were business-oriented. Continental sold tires and a host of rubber products, including water hoses, coats, bathing caps, and tennis balls. The clever material Remarque wrote and edited soliciting buyers for Continental's products included cartoons based on Max and Moritz, the beloved German forerunners of the American comic strip "The Katzenjammer Kids"; sketches linking travel and the automobile; and an essay in which Remarque defended automakers' prices to customers who might refuse to buy automobiles. Most of Remarque's work on the *Echo Continental* did not survive the bombing raids over Hannover during the Second World War. The content and style of the few surviving issues of this trade journal, from 1923–24, hold no great surprises for Remarque scholars. The apprentice writer, it seems, was cutting his teeth on advertising copy and travel-related business promotional literature at the dawn of that genre of writing. Another benefit of Remarque's position with a trade journal—a job he kept until 1925—was being able to make professional contacts with other editors.

In 1925 Remarque moved to Berlin and became a picture editor for *Sport im Bild* (Sport in Pictures), a Berlin Scherl Verlag journal aimed at car owners and racing car drivers of the monied upper class. Making the move from Hannover with him was a work colleague from *Echo Continental*, Jutta Ilse Zambona, whom he married on 14 October 1925 (Mynona, 253). In addition to working for *Bild*, Remarque contributed many articles to other Scherl magazines and newspapers (Mynona, 256). In Berlin Remarque was in a position to accept or reject manuscript submissions, a role that made him a shining star and man-about-town in Berlin's vibrant publishing industry. He and his wife moved freely through the night life of the city's bars and cabarets. Axel Eggebrecht, who would interview Remarque in 1929 for the journal *Die Literarische Welt* (The Literary World), recalls in his autobiography *Der halbe Weg* (Halfway, 1975) that, as Remarque became a world celebrity, he was not adverse to an "open marriage" with his wife.[3] Eggebrecht's book offers an interesting dimension to the still blurry picture of Remarque's working life in Berlin during the Weimar Republic; Eggebrecht criticizes Remarque's self-appointed role as a popularizer of democratic and humanistic values.

A brief look at Remarque's articles for *Bild* reveals a group of topics more varied than those he covered for the *Echo Continental*: automobile accidents, safety on the road, new automobile literature, traffic on city streets, even the particular interests and concerns of women drivers. Remarque was a lifelong enthusiast of the emerging automobile technology and also bought and traded expensive cars. One interesting *Bild* piece is his short prose sketch "Das Rennen Vanderveldes" (Vanderveldes's Race), which he originally submitted from Hannover. He later expanded "Race" into a novel that would be serialized in *Bild* under the title *Station am Horizont* (Station on the Horizon, 1927–28). *Station*, in turn, would undergo several adaptations: it was the basis for Remarque's novel *Heaven Has No Favorites* (1961), as well as for two American feature films, *The Other Love* (1947) and *Bobby Deerfield* (1977). The race car driver Vandervelde appears as Kai in *Station* and later as Clerfayt in *Heaven*. Vandervelde, Kai, and Clerfayt are stock romantic heroes, similar to those found in most magazine fiction of the early modern industrial era. International settings in Italy and on the French Riviera would appear in *Station*; such backgrounds in his early fiction were based on Remarque's own business trips as an editor to the European playgrounds of "the rich and famous." The same woman, Lillian, chooses Vandervelde in one story and Kai in the other as her lover. A sense of déjà vu pervades the Vandervelde and Clerfayt stories. The two feature film adaptations and three prose versions of this racing car romance are good examples of Remarque's facile ability to rework sellable material and craft it into art, an ability he would retain as a mature writer.

A close reading of *Dream Room* and *Station* suggests their thematic origins in the fashionable turn-of-the-century ideas of Arthur Schopenhauer, Friedrich Nietzsche, and Oswald Spengler. Pessimism, art, mythology, and the fall of Western culture were attractive themes for all levels of serious German artists. As a struggling young writer, Remarque absorbed the ideas emanating from the texts of Germany's aging cultural icons. If *Dream Room* salutes a popular Nietzschean vision of the artist as a Dionysian individualist (Fritz Schramm), then *Station*'s Kai is a romantic figure from modernist Europe, marked by Spengler's stoicism and his notion of life as a matter of "renewable" experiences. As racing car drivers, Kai and Clerfayt move from one level of physical and spiritual achievement to another. For Kai, racing cars symbolize a pragmatic way of overcoming the sterility of bourgeois cultural structures. He describes his life as "center-directed"; he does not live on the periphery. But life as described in both *Dream Room* and *Station* revolves around the viability of individual experience, the élan vital of personal discovery and survivability.

Despite these philosophical overtones, Remarque would never achieve the same rank as a philosopher-writer as, for instance, Hermann Hesse in *Das Glasperlenspiel* (*Magister Ludi*, 1949), or Thomas Mann in *Der Zauberberg* (The Magic Mountain, 1927). Remarque found an early voice as a literary transmitter of ideology derived from the concepts of popular German philosophy. He never claimed to have done more. Early texts like *Dream Room* focus on the "sublime" vitalistic experience as an antidote to inactivity and the death of sensual development. But such an antidote is only superficially an attractive response to the profundity of human existence. Nietzsche's thought appears in *Dream Room* as only a pale reflection of that philosopher's aesthetic program on the origins of art and the character of the artist. And the racing car as a metaphor of life is hardly constructive or even workable as an answer to personal suffering and despair.

Remarque's philosophical limitations do not diminish, however, the value of his insights into the motivations behind the heroic actions of unknown men and women, whom he rewards with the gift of belief in their own heroism. Heroism is, of course, a central theme of *All Quiet*.

# 5

# Autobiographical Sources

## NARRATIVE SUMMARY OF THE NOVEL

Paul Bäumer, an 18-year-old German recruit, is at rest five miles behind the western front. Like his comrades, he is part of a reserve unit with the German army during World War I. It is summer 1917. Paul and his friends dream of family and home and have not given up hope for an end to the war.

In recording Bäumer's thoughts and reflections about civil and military authority, the book conveys the self-evident falsehood of the idealism of war. In chapters 4 through 6 the reader follows Bäumer into combat, a "mysterious whirlpool" (AQ, 52) punctured by the sound of French rockets and dying horses. Bäumer moves through the Battle of Flanders, guided by Kat, his mentor, and undergoes his first encounter with the enemy on the front. War becomes an authentic, survivable experience. He is granted leave and a short pass to go home, where he will visit his family, especially his sick mother. The estrangement between his father and himself creates tension and silence. Neither father nor son can talk about lingering, unresolved emotional issues. The war exacerbates their already distant relationship. Chapters 8 and 9 stress Bäumer's growing insight into war as a human and national tragedy. He has two further encounters with the enemy: at home, when he visits a camp for Russian prisoners, and back on the front line, when he kills a French soldier, Duval. These two singular episodes turn the enemy into brothers and fellow sufferers. Military propagandists on both sides, Bäumer feels, have done a good job of concealing the human cost of the conflict.

Bäumer's tragic insight into his predicament—that he is trapped and that war is an absurdist experience for the common man, regardless of military rank or nationality—becomes a private revelation with which knowledge he dies anonymously on the front, "almost glad," as Remarque notes, that "the end had come" (*AQ*, 248). The brief epilogue notes that on that particular day the German war office told the country there was nothing new to report from the western front. Such a communiqué was, of course, the daily deceptive message for the German people. *Im Westen nichts Neues* (All Quiet on the Western Front) became the title of Remarque's war novel. The moral hypocrisy and irony of that military report is self-evident throughout the text.

# THE ROLE OF AUTOBIOGRAPHICAL SOURCES IN *ALL QUIET ON THE WESTERN FRONT*

Among Remarque's immediate sources for *All Quiet* were his personal experiences: memories of his family life in Osnabrück and of his military service, spent with his classmates from the teachers' seminar. There are also references to particular places: Osnabrück street names and buildings, the *Pappelgraben* (poplar canal). *All Quiet* thus achieves a level of authenticity related to key years of Remarque's life; what emerges is a war novel that hovers between fact and fiction.

The text, however, is not pure autobiography, and the reader might remember that Goethe called his own autobiography "poetry and truth." Nevertheless, after persistent searching, the writer Hanns-

Gerd Rabe turned up some important autobiographical underpinnings to *All Quiet*. Despite many obstacles—including Remarque's uncertain cooperation—Rabe managed to establish a fundamental chronology of the personal and cultural events reflected in the novel. An awareness of these events is basic to any understanding of the novel, as well as of the continuing critical debate over the merits of war fiction and military memoirs of the Great War.

Remarque's book has not escaped this debate. The public might reasonably expect that a writer of war fiction has had experience as a combatant. Remarque met this requirement inasmuch as he experienced the outbreak of the Battle of Flanders, but Rabe notes that his exposure to combat was brief (1970, 214). The professional soldier would consider service and length of time on the battlefield in assessing any war novel or a memoir—hence the charge leveled against Remarque that his novel was more fiction than fact. In 1929 conservative Germans seem to have preferred a war novel written by a career soldier. Nevertheless, there is now little doubt that, however brief, Remarque's war experience (viewed through time and memory) was an essential contribution to his book.

**Remarque as Paul Bäumer**     The first name of Remarque's major character, Paul, comes from Remarque's own birth certificate: Erich Paul Remark. Paul's surname is that of Remarque's maternal grandmother, Adelheid Bäumer. There are other direct family references in *All Quiet*. Remarque's (sick) mother, along with his father and younger sister, Erna, appear as characters in chapters 7 and 8, when Bäumer gets leave to return home. And home is Osnabrück. Erna, who in the novel is making potato pancakes when Bäumer surprises her in the kitchen, was destined to be Remarque's only surviving sister after his older sister Elfriede was executed by the Nazis for treason (Rabe 1970, 201). (A street in Osnabrück is named after her.)  Another important family reference in *All Quiet* concerns the dying French soldier, Duval. Bäumer discovers that Duval, like his father, was a typographer. The intensity of emotion displayed by Bäumer when he makes this discovery raises questions, admittedly speculative, about unresolved problems between Remarque and his own father. Remarque made a special point of returning to Osnabrück for his father's funeral on 9 June 1954.

These several allusions to family members occur at the end of the novel. There is little reason, however, to believe that in 1929 Remarque's readers were aware of the extent to which he had used family memories and references. These family references underline the desperation of German civilians living behind the front line, especially the poor, who suffered great material deprivation. Remarque includes a touching and realistic scene in which Bäumer's father worries about the cost of his wife's cancer operation. Bäumer senses that the old man is too proud and ashamed to ask the doctor about the bill. His father fears that the doctor will misinterpret the question.

An equally important autobiographical link is that between Bäumer's soldier comrades and Remarque's friends from the interrupted teachers' seminar. They are essentially one and the same group. The fate of Bäumer's reserve unit was a common one, and as Bäumer, Remarque speaks for the "class of 1898," an estranged generation commandeered by the Great War. Chapter 1 describes the differences between the young combatants in this war and their elders, a generation gap defined by more than age. Not only did the older generation, builders of an empire, betray the younger one in subverting the much bruited German ideals of civic and military authority, but the horror of viewing their first deaths on the battlefield shattered the youthful belief that age brings wisdom. Such speculation in Bäumer's group leads them inevitably to challenge German notions of heroism. Bäumer shares something special with his comrades—academic education. He and his friends cannot fail to perceive the failure of that education to resolve the glaring contradictions between the theory and practice of German ideals.

## Remarque's Military Training and Combat Experience

Though the First World War began in August 1914, Remarque did not enlist until 26 November 1916. Three members of his seminar had joined two years earlier, and one can only assume that their teachers pressured Remarque and his classmates to follow suit. German teachers, of whatever rank or station, viewed themselves as servants of the state, model figures in German society who followed the party line. In due course, Remarque and his group began basic training at the well-known Caprivikaserne (Caprivi Barracks) located on the Westerberg, a chain of hills northwest of Osnabrück (Rabe 1970, 210). As Bäumer, Remarque recalls this bitter period in the first chapter; he notes that it was a time when the boot brush mattered, not the mind. Recruits were taught to put their intelligence aside and follow the military system. Drilling soldiers into a unit was the goal. Bäumer remembers his anger at having to suffer under the hands of Corporal Himmelstoss, a former postman (AQ, 26). Himmelstoss, whose main argument with Bäumer and other recruits was their air of defiance against his rank, is destined to meet them once again on the western front.

Remarque left the Caprivi Barracks to undergo more training at a military camp in Celle, northeast of Osnabrück in the Luneburg Heath, a historic tourist area south of Hannover. Remarque's mother became seriously ill at this time. From Celle, Remarque went to the western front, in Belgium, on 14 July 1917. He joined the second company of the field recruit depot of the Second Guard Reserve Division. This division was stationed in the region of Ham-Lenglet on the Canal de la Sensée, behind the Arras front. Trenches and dugouts stretched off into the horizon, a characteristic war zone landscape. Remarque and his comrades were then transported by rail to Flanders, where they waited out the British and French attack on the German forces.

The Battle of Flanders was conceived and conducted under the efficient but eccentric leadership of Field Marshall Douglas Haig, commander of the British army. Most historians agree that Haig decided on the offensive as a one-man effort to win the war before the Americans arrived in Europe. Though Haig had been advised against it, his plan developed into a dubious "vision" of certain victory. His decision was out of touch with military intelligence. There was, in fact, no credible threat of a major German offensive in 1917, especially after the Germans had been impressed by the tenacity of the French at Verdun in 1916. The Germans had chosen to withdraw and recuperate, so they were surprised to be drawn so quickly into a new conflict. Haig's offensive was launched on 31 July 1917 with over 3,000 guns firing four and a half million shells. The Battle of Flanders was destined to end on 6 November in the village of Passchendaele in an expanse of mud. The rain-swollen landscape was symbolic of Haig's futile attempt to confront the enemy.

But Passchendaele lay in the future. German reserve units, similar to those of the Second Guard Reserve Division in Flanders, were expected to do most of the fighting against the British, whose commanders had put their army into an untenable position. Remarque was a sapper (military engineer) in a unit whose duty was repairing and supplying wire fences, bunkers, and trenches. Chapter 4 of *All Quiet* contains several direct references to this activity—for instance, in the opening sentence Remarque notes that the men have to go up on wiring fatigue (49). Bäumer's companions on the front line are almost all familiar faces from Remarque's Osnabrück teachers' seminar, and the majority are introduced in the first chapter; some of their names have been changed for fiction, and some have not. Rabe mentions the following: Katschinsky (Kat in the novel), Detering (Detering), Seppel Oelfke (Haie Westhus), Georg Middendorf (Albert Kropp), and Theo Troske (Troske) (Rabe 1970, 211). First names of the first two original sources are not available in Rabe. Kat is especially important to Bäumer, and Remarque shows the two men fighting alongside each other and sharing food found on abandoned farmland. The Bäumer-Kat relationship defines best what Remarque calls military comradeship, for him the greatest lesson of the Great War. Remarque's soldiers are a mixture of North German fishermen, blue-collar workers, and former students in the Osnabrück teachers' seminar; their bond is forged in the context of the emotional and social adaptations required by the ever present danger of death in combat. War for these plain men is normal, but they do not like it. The friendships among Remarque's men in *All Quiet* are true and convincing because of the realistic portrayal of their enlisted men's status; war for them, in the words of the reviewer Henry Seidel Canby, is an "existence, to be described as one might describe any other hazardous occupation, such as coal mining" (1088). These soldiers, ordinarily despised by the German upper classes as disposable hostages, have an astounding lucidity of judgment. Their hardiness (in Bäumer's eyes) leads to an end that the officer caste cannot accept: the German enlisted man's grievance against the political and military machine.

Changes occur during wartime, especially to man's evolving definition of morality. This is pointedly illustrated in a central episode of chapter 1 in which Bäumer agrees to let his friend Müller take a pair of boots from Kemmerich, who is dying in a hospital ward from an amputated leg (*AQ*, 21). Bäumer, who loves Kemmerich like a brother, knows that he will never leave the hospital alive, and that establishing ownership of his boots after his death is a crucial issue. Kemmerich firsts asks Müller for the boots but Müller hesitates. Bäumer will later conceal the facts of Kemmerich's death from the dead soldier's mother, who wants to think her son died a hero.

An outstanding mentor and teacher for Bäumer in the early months of the conflict is Kat, a 40-year-old peasant "with the face of the soil" (*AQ*, 9) a shrewd man with a knack for finding food in abandoned farmhouses. He is described by Remarque as the natural leader of Bäumer's immediate group. A crude and vulgar man, Kat is at the center of the episodes censored in *All Quiet*'s first American edition. Kat is an armchair philosopher as well, one who offers the novel's best insights into the correlation between enlisted men and the abuse of military authority. Kat asserts that an insignificant man in civilian life is easily corrupted by the gift of military power over others. In *All Quiet* Himmelstoss and Kantorek, the latter based on a teacher-soldier from the Osnabrück teachers' seminar, are both stunning examples of Kat's thesis that "little men" enjoy the abuse of power. As a prototype of the servile academic, Kantorek corrupts the spirit of German patriotism. His phrase "the Iron Youth"—an abuse of the phrase "the Iron Cross"—recurs throughout the text as a leitmotiv that parodies the status quo and foreshadows the failure of Bäumer's unit to come out of the war alive.

At an important point in the tenth chapter, autobiography and fiction coalesce; the episode includes the first reference in the text to Bäumer's being wounded by enemy shells. This reference begins with the words "you are lost," and then the following: "A blow sweeps like a whip over my left leg. I hear Albert cry out" (*AQ*, 204). Bäumer and his comrades, including Albert Kropp, are evacuating a village when the enemy begins to fire on everybody. After they are hit, Bäumer and Kropp manage to hide and then call out to a passing ambulance. They are picked up and taken to a medical dressing station. Bäumer is sent to a hospital, where he will undergo an operation. Remarque was wounded differently: while out on wiring fatigue duty east of the Houthulst Forest south of Handzaeme, on the first day of the Battle of Flanders (31 July 1917), he was injured by shell fragments; his wounds were to his neck, left leg above the knee, and upper right arm. He was picked up by his friend Georg Middendorf, along with six other wounded soldiers. Middendorf made the following entry in his diary on 31 July: "There were [other injured men], among them . . . Remarque. . . . I bandaged him but did not see any heavy wounds" (Rabe 1970, 212). Remarque was taken to a central gathering place, Geite-Sankt-Josef, then to a field hospital in Thourout, and finally to St. Vincenz Hospital (still in operation to this day) in Duisburg (in northern Germany). Remarque arrived in Duisburg in the middle of August 1917.

In chapter 10 Bäumer convalesces at a "Catholic hospital" analogous to St. Vincenz. His observations brilliantly capture the hospital's sardonic staff of doctors and their assistants, the nuns. Bäumer criticizes extensively, however, those surgeons and others in the medical profession for whom the war is "a glorious time." As doctors operate on them, soldiers endure the horror of amputation. To see what war is, one need look no further than a military hospital, says Bäumer at an especially low point in his recuperation. He describes the enforced period of treatment as a torture chamber, as it was in other hospitals in Germany, France, and Russia. Hospitals do not cure or heal but make suffering refined and heroic. At this point *All Quiet* comes closest to matching the mood and tenor of another famous war novel, the French writer Henri Barbusse's *Under Fire* (1918), based on his trench diaries and written while he was in hospital. It is in a hospital as a recuperating patient that the narrators of both *Under Fire* and *All Quiet* further question the experience of war, having experienced it from the personal level of pain and suffering.

Remarque was released from St. Vincenz Hospital on 31 October 1918. He had not seen combat for a year. He was ordered to return to

Osnabrück for garrison duty and was duly assigned to the First Replacement Battalion of Infantry Regiment 78. On 7 November he was examined by the battalion doctor and declared fit for return to the front. Four days later, however, the war ended and an armistice was declared. The kaiser left Germany and crossed the border into Holland. Remarque was no longer a soldier, and he returned home to the chaotic social and political conditions of the "November Revolution" and other events that seriously threatened the stability of the former German empire. No military records exist that indicate the exact date of Remarque's discharge from service. The autobiographical elements of his next book, *The Road Back* (1931), continue *All Quiet*'s autobiographical sequences, which effectively conclude with chapter 10.

# CONCLUSION

In *All Quiet* Remarque incorporated and transformed two of his own lasting impressions of the war: his wounding by shell fragments on 31 July, and his encounters with sick and dying soldiers in medical stations near the front line. Their origin in his own battlefield experience probably accounts for the truly effective portrayal of these key events in the novel and their impact on the reader. It is interesting to note that these autobiographical elements are not as specific as one might expect. For example, any reader who is a trained soldier, as Rabe notes, can see that in the wounding scene Remarque neither describes a specific attack nor gives details of a particular battle, such as the Battle of Flanders (1970, 214). Only latter-day scholarship has uncovered the site and date of Remarque's wounding; it is not at all apparent from the text of *All Quiet*. Remarque depicts Bäumer's wounding in a generalized, abstract setting, an anonymous village, and devotes only five pages of text to the incident of his wounding and subsequent transport to a field hospital. Bäumer's recuperation at the Catholic hospital, on the other hand, covers the remainder of chapter 10, which includes an elaborately reconstructed account of his hospital experience that mixes fiction and fact in such a way that the reader succombs to lighter aspects of an otherwise fearful episode in the  war.

Yet as he wrote *All Quiet* ten years later, with not only little time for research and considering the brevity of his own direct encounter with the enemy on the western front, little personal battlefield knowledge, Remarque wisely resorted to reconstructing the facts of war fictionally rather than with documentary accuracy. Indeed, such factual records are best left to the generals and officers of combat. *All Quiet* is not a war novel in which the military facts are always verifiable. As war fiction, however, it is as convincing as any autobiography. Remarque was more talented as an artist than a historian, and his realistic descriptions of battle scenes are nevertheless selective and impressionistic—even those details and events that are grounded in his own life.

# 6

## Aspects of a Literary Style

A meaningful analysis of style in *All Quiet* is tantamount to a definition of the author as a writer and figure reflective of his time and place. Literary style may denote simply an author's specific choice of words, sentence structures, and figures of speech, but nonlinguistic factors, not always perceptible to the reader, can also influence it. Style can reflect a particular culture; one can speak of an American literary style as opposed to a German one. Literary style is always related to the "high" ("truth" and "beauty") or "low" (incest) standing of a topic or subject. Finally, literary style often indicates the particular reading audience an author is addressing.

An essential component of the style of *All Quiet* is the novel's status as an early twentieth-century text, whose subject is the recent European conflict. A reader might expect the language and tone to reflect the historical and cultural period 1914–18, but instead the language—cast in the historical present tense—and style are vibrant and immediate. Remarque's first audience in 1929 was German, but his book addressed many other potential readers. France, England, and the United States had fought in the recent conflict and were likewise evaluating the Great War in works of fiction.

Through the direct, simple and affecting language of his protagonist, Paul Bäumer, Remarque transmitted his pacifist sentiments about
ending all wars. The words and language in *All Quiet* cross social and
linguistic boundaries. The educated German Left failed, however, to
find in Remarque's book the passionate leftist language calling for
social and political revolution. Since the novel was never intended to
be a political manifesto or even a militaristic tract, it was clear to
socialists and communists that Remarque was neither a leftist comrade
nor an apologist for a "white man's war." Remarque's language conveyed rather a dominant authorial tone of sentimental, introspective
self-expression. The literary style of *All Quiet* identifies expressively
with the suffering and distress of the enlisted man's social class. In contrast to the language of Ernst Jünger's German officer spokesman in
his war novel *The Storm of Steel*, Bäumer's words and thoughts are
devoid of aesthetic, tortured fabrication. *All Quiet*'s language never
approaches Jünger's rhetoric, in which war is a vehicle of rebirth for
mankind and the German national ethos, a Nietzschean image of the
triumph of reason and beauty through chaos. When Bäumer substi-
tutes the language of "We" for the language of "I," doing so subsumes
his identity into the communal speech and language of his comrades
on the front. In this sense, Bäumer is more "advanced" in expressive
concepts of social unity and class solidarity than the frenzied pamphle-
teers among the German leftists of the 1920s, who attacked the style
of *All Quiet* as only vaguely sympathetic to class conflict. The direct
emotion and tragic experience conveyed by Paul Bäumer's own words
become a singularly affecting witness to the failure of civic and military
leadership in the Great War.

*All Quiet* is predominantly impressionistic in style, even in those
several scenes that clearly relate to everyday reality. Bäumer's language
reflects both the impressionism and the reality of a soldier at war; it is
rooted in body functions, food, sex, and combat. Bäumer's visit home
is realistically and impressionistically portrayed, as is his recuperation
in a military hospital. But one searches in vain for conventional touch-
stones of realism; Remarque's realism continually drifts toward
impressionism, an artistic style that tries to convey to the reader (the
receptor) the essential "mental" impression that an event or individual

has made upon the central character. In the novel sentiments and impressions are rendered first through Bäumer's eyes and then through Remarque's medium, the language of literary impressions. Bäumer's language induces an impressionistic state of mind in the reader. The linkage between words and thoughts, or between sight and words, is thus inescapable. The realistic details normally found in the context of war recede into a dreamlike background, but they are, in fact, manipulated by Remarque artistically and aesthetically. Bäumer's experience of war becomes finally a series of images of that war. Critics have glibly labeled Remarque's impressionist style as facile and romantic, thereby implying that he had minimal experience of the reality of war. It is, however, much more to the point to accept his language as a subjective, impressionistic account of combat experience.

Remarque, who later became a collector of masterpieces of the French impressionists (Degas, Pissaro, Renoir), made the early decision in writing *All Quiet* to "paint" impressions of war in words, even if in doing so he sacrificed a sense of authenticity and whatever others chose to call reality in artistic expression.[1] The following discussion is intended not only to point out the variety of literary styles to be found in selected chapters of *All Quiet* but to illuminate Remarque's purposeful methodology in linking literary function and style.

## CHAPTER ONE

This expository chapter introduces all the important aspects of the novel: its setting, characters, and central social and political issues. Language here serves a reporting, descriptive, and practical function. The first word of the novel is *We*, not *I*. The narrator, Paul Bäumer, chooses to stress his identity as part of a group. Describing his comrades in war, Tjaden, Müller, Kropp, and others, comes before any delineation of individual identity. For instance, Tjaden has "voracity," and Müller uses "foresight" (*AQ*, 7). Haie Westhus is a peat digger, and Detering is a peasant. All that the reader learns about the current location of the group is that it is five miles behind the front (*AQ*, 7). Unlike more documentary-style war novels, *All Quiet* is perennially nonspecific about location, a stylistic trademark that enhances its subjective qualities as a work of fiction.

In the opening chapter the men talk personally to one another; in fact, some of the most affecting passages are those in which the simple words of soldiers reveal the emotional warmth of unadorned language. Tjaden "begs" for food from the company cook—the beans look good cooked with meat and fat. Army talk may induce closeness, but it is clear that Remarque's soldiers are as intimately connected to their stomachs and intestines as to other men. A censored episode in the first American edition of *All Quiet* describes in detail a "wonderful day" for Bäumer and his comrades—they are able to spend two hours on latrine boxes scattered about an empty field (*AQ*, 12). The boxes are described as a happy substitute for common toilets. The latrine interlude is a splendid and farcical opportunity for the reader to learn that a soldier's language comes (appropriately) from his lower regions. An enlisted man's most passionate indignation and anger are used, besides fighting, in the service of preserving his free time in the latrine. A "latrine-rumor" is a wonderfully descriptive army word that refers to talk and gossip shared in the common space of a latrine. The literary style of this episode points up what polite society prefers to conceal, and Remarque achieves this effect by juxtaposing images: the flowery meadow, the windblown hair—of men responding to the call of nature.

As stylistic devices, report and description in a novel are often related to the author's use of time. Remarque's lengthy, detailed descriptions of interactions between people take up more time than his frequently undetailed reports of fighting on the field. Those pages of chapter 1 that describe Bäumer's visit to the hospital bed of his friend Kemmerich are extended and broad (*AQ*, 17–22). Not only does the reader learn the impact of Kemmerich's expected death on the military supplies of Bäumer's unit, but these pages also convey Bäumer's fanciful, impressionistic images of death "working through" Kemmerich's body: after his death Kemmerich's fingernails will continue to grow as etiolated cellar plants; "death" will continue to live from cells from the wider realm of life. These are prototypical romantic images stressing horror and subjective fear of death. Remarque also introduces allusions from European Gothic literature: hair growing on a dead man's skull, waxlike hands on Death the Grim Reaper (*AQ*, 18). In the meantime, Bäumer notes that Kemmerich is being given a shot of morphine to relieve his suffering, and the reader, along with Bäumer, reenters the "real" world. The stylistic effect on the reader of this extended impressionistic episode is the skillful manipulation of his or her feelings and sensibilities. Remarque creates an emotional mood of depression, horror, and fatality, as well as an aesthetic rendering of Death.

# CHAPTER FOUR

Chapter 4 is divided into eight sections, each of which displays a different literary style. The first section is descriptive. Army trucks have arrived to gather men for wiring fatigue duty (*AQ*, 49). There is unrelenting engine noise and continual movement toward the front, on roads that are old and need to be repaired, as munition columns march parallel to the trucks. These are classic images of soldiers and equipment in the Great War: men walked, and guns were carried on foot whenever possible, even for great distances. Bäumer and his comrades can hear the sounds of cackling geese at nearby farmhouses; they can smell smoke and taste gunpowder on their tongues. Remarque uses a simile to describe hidden gun positions: they "look like a kind of military Feast of Tabernacles" (*AQ*, 50). Kat, the seasoned veteran, feels that the English will bomb the Germans that night.

Suddenly, Remarque's realistic landscape becomes subjective and impressionistic. As enlisted men approach the immediate zone of the front, they seem to anticipate their initial contact with the imminent danger. Dying (or the threat of death) changes a man's physiology. Fear induces alertness, sensual arousal, and readiness, as though the front itself were an electric current that activates nerve centers. Thus far, Remarque has described the initial sensations of war, its irresistible pull toward a vortex of abandonment, a self-sacrifice to a power greater than oneself. The second section of the chapter, in rhetorical and stylized language, describes the sustaining forces of "air" and "earth" that always conspire to awaken a preservation instinct in man, even on the western front. Bäumer says that a soldier is continually reminded that the earth will either kill or save a man. Remarque calls this knowledge a "second sight." Trenches and ditches can protect a fighting man from flying shell fragments. Earth is a friend, a brother, and a mother: "We, thy redeemed ones, bury ourselves in thee" (*AQ*, 53).

From the metaphor of the earth as a protecting mother, Remarque moves stylistically to a major impressionistic image: the front as a panorama of colored sensations. When the front line emerges, Bäumer first sees an ambiguous red glow from one end of the skyline to the other. The redness is broken by battery fire, silver and red circles coming down as stars in colors of red, white, and green. The parachute of a French rocket drops gracefully to the ground. Shells remind Bäumer again of wild birds. This theatrically colorful picture of the front is illuminated by the beams of huge searchlights moving across the sky. Besides colors and selective imagery, Remarque also uses hearing and sound in a special way to reinforce the impressionism of this vision. At one point in the fourth section of this chapter, wounded and dying horses must be shot. Their anguish and suffering are loud and clear. The analogy to the sound of dying soldiers is unavoidable for the reader, but as one soldier remarks, men must be looked after first and the horses killed later. Remarque places the sound of the groaning animals somewhere in a "great silvery landscape." As effective as these passages are artistically, the distinctive language and finely tuned sensations of Remarque's stylistic impressionism seem to prevail over the requirements for producing a realistic warfare setting.

The concluding sections of chapter 4 feature Bäumer and his comrades taking cover from enemy shells in a graveyard covered by black crosses. The graveyard symbol is inescapable. Young German soldiers have come to die in the logical final resting place. The cemetery is also the melodramatic setting for battle. There is a first and then a second explosion of shell fire. The graveyard is, ironically, the only available cover when the men are suddenly caught between the open fields and the burial mounds. The fields, Remarque notes, are a "surging sea," and Bäumer suffers surface wounds when he crawls into an uprooted coffin for protection (*AQ*, 61). He lies next to a dead man.

There is a brief respite from surface shelling, but this interlude in the bombardment is followed by the next obstacle facing Bäumer and his unit—gas. Men swoon and expire from fear and surprise. Only Kat, the army veteran, knows how to escape death from gas.

This entire episode, like so many others in the text, is rendered primarily from Bäumer's point of view. The emphasis is on the dramatic, stagelike setting (a cemetery), the border line between life and death (war as a backdrop conducive to death). Bäumer's language is reflective and philosophical in tone. When the graveyard becomes a pile of "wreckage," the coffins and their contents scattered about, these earlier corpses are killed a "second time" (AQ, 65). Their "dying" again, however, provides salvation for every German soldier who crawls into an open coffin. Thus far, Bäumer's encounter with death on the battlefield has been expressed in an inner monologue (the reader is present) underscored by the moods and sensations of the experience itself. Bäumer's sensitivity contrasts with the bovine perceptions of those German enlisted men who are content to do no more than fight.

# CHAPTER SIX

Chapter 6 accelerates Bäumer's depression and melancholy about the war and contains two episodes that underline both his and Remarque's growing pessimism about the outcome of the conflict. There are references once more to a generation set emotionally adrift by the war—specifically, to what has been lost by Bäumer's comrades in the course of the conflict. Bäumer himself has learned to kill, and his generation has lost all fellow feeling. They are like walking dead "who . . . are still able to run and to kill" (AQ, 102). Kill or be killed is a primary lesson of war. Fighting and killing are defenses against disappearance and annihilation; moreover, killing satisfies a basic need for revenge. A murderer, Bäumer remembers, kills for release against a greater evil. The lost generation has confronted and accepted the rational use of killing as a defense of one's life. After such an emotional upheaval, however, Bäumer's essential business is to try to become something like a man, a human being, again. He gets this chance one night while standing sentry duty.

This second telling episode in chapter 6 makes a statement about Bäumer's sensitivity to the loss of his irretrievable past. On a particular evening, images of his youth overcome those of war and killing, and Bäumer seems happy to succumb to a personal memory of former times. These images of home are ushered in by soaring parachute lights that "dissolve" into a cathedral cloister; in this memory of tranquillity, plants are blooming in a quadrangle and Bäumer, not yet 20, is dreaming of love (*AQ*, 105). An exploding shell on the front line announces the entry of another "picture" of the past (Remarque also uses the word *apparitions* to reinforce the otherworldly beauty of these impressions), an avenue lined with poplars in the suburbs of Osnabrück. To Bäumer's surprise, however, these peaceful memories of the past arouse in him sorrow rather than desire and melancholy. It turns out that war has killed his feelings and desires; they are long gone and survive only as artifacts from another world. Bäumer's pessimistic reflections give deeper meaning to this mournful episode about the nature of loss and displacement in war. Visions of utter beauty fail to retrieve the past as death and dying on the front take over.

Emotional intimacy with the past, Remarque believes, is impossible for men who have learned to make hard distinctions and cruel decisions, whose sensitivity and higher sentiments have been replaced by indifference and atrophy. On occasion, however, Bäumer's wartime landscape is touched by unexpected encounters with images of the serendipity of nature. These are events over which man has no control, and as such they are welcomed, for the enigma of their appearance is a sign of divine intervention. One such episode occurs toward the end of the sixth chapter, when Bäumer notes that two butterflies are playing in front of a trench (*AQ*, 112). With no plants or flowers in sight, the butterflies land on a skull. This image is highly effective as an allegory that links several levels of meaning; especially cogent at this time to Bäumer is the linkage between life and death, between beauty and terror. The butterflies are likewise an allusion to the transitory existence of man.

# CHAPTERS EIGHT AND NINE

The literary style of *All Quiet*, its earliest critics on the Right noted, is intentionally subversive politically. Remarque never denied the pacifist tenor of *All Quiet*; nevertheless, such readers claimed that his language goes beyond mere condemnation of war. It is always rewarding to find those parts of his novel where the style inverts the jingoistic mythology of war by highlighting certain incidents, thereby drawing the reader's attention. These incidents reflect the author's point of view.

Two such antiwar episodes (one each in chapters 7 and 8) serve to undermine traditional German ideas about the special nature of war and the sense of comradeship and communality it supposedly promotes. According to such notions, one consolation war provides the soldier facing death, a refuge against fear, is the support of his comrades on the line. Even in a world defined by the hard rules of military combat, a soldier's comrades are always his compatriots. Remarque reworks this idea in chapter 7 when his language undermines the official distinction between comrades and enemies. Bäumer, home on leave, is standing guard over Russian prisoners of war. He observes their "foreign" faces and begins to notice that their foreheads, noses, and mouths "look just as kindly as [those of] our own peasants in Friesland" (*AQ*, 163). Not only does Bäumer see physical resemblances between native Germans and the Russian prisoners of war, but he is willing to extend the warmth of comradeship to the enemy. He reasons that German soldiers on enemy soil might be similarly standing next to one another, the image of pathetic creatures, breathing the wind blowing through the fields and forests of a foreign country. At this point Bäumer does not dare to move beyond German military law's definitions of friend and foe. But his thoughts are free, and Bäumer opts to empathize with the suffering, the melancholy, and the pitifulness of the human condition within the context of war. Bäumer thus breaks through controlled, propagandistic language, especially that line of demarcation between "comrade" and "enemy."

If this episode in chapter 7 introduces a radical redefinition of comradeship—one based on shared humanity rather than on patriotism—a related incident occurs in chapter 8, when Bäumer, on the front line, is forced to choose between intrinsic and patriotic values, between subjective principles and national and ethnic precepts. Bäumer is part of a patrol for which he has volunteered. Once all of the unit is over the front line, they agree to split up and move forward separately; Bäumer, however, finds he cannot go any further and is paralyzed by fear. Moving forward or not becomes a test of German comradeship and unit loyalty and hence a test of the principle of patriotism. Bäumer tells himself he must leave the hollow, where, as an independent person, he has made a stand not to take an active part in the fighting on the front line. He is temporarily "saved" from this condition by the sound of his comrades' voices conveying familiar "comforts" that, through their nearness, promise to realease him from the fear of death (*AQ*, 182). Bäumer seems to have conquered his ego and surrendered to the higher cause of preserving his self-respect and dignity. At this point, however, a falling body lands on Bäumer as he crouches in a shell hole, and his first impulse is only to protect himself. He hits "madly home"—he kills instinctively.

This act is a discovery for Bäumer on several levels (*AQ*, 185). He realizes that he has killed a man, that someone else's death is his doing, and he is forced to confront the suffering of that person's slow dying. There follows a long monologue in which Bäumer makes his confession, in almost subversive terms. He tells the Frenchman—a printer named Gerard Duval, a common soldier like Bäumer himself—that he did not want to kill him. Bäumer addresses the dying soldier as a comrade rather than as an abstract enemy. How could a poor Frenchman be his enemy, he asks, a man with a common background characterized by poverty and social suffering? This experience gives Bäumer cathartic insight into the brotherhood of all men.

Duval's death at the hands of Bäumer marks a major turning point in the antiwar language of the novel; from this point on, Bäumer's consciousness is truly and profoundly radicalized. The reader has no problem apprehending the terror and pathos of Remarque's rhetoric against war. Bäumer's inner change is effected by a direct encounter with the enemy, an unexpected epiphany that enables him to overcome German military rhetoric and shallow patriotism. Remarque's literary style verbalizes both his and Bäumer's grief over the nonviability of war. The rest of Bäumer's company unit goes on with the conventional business of war while Bäumer becomes a tragic figure, precisely because he is working his way through all aspects of the war experience.

## CONCLUSION

In the concluding chapters of *All Quiet* the style moves from the naturalistic tone of chapter 10 to the language of Bäumer's elegiac, mournful sense that his "superfluous" life is coming to an end in a shameful conflict. The style of the novel begins to reflect his loss of dignity, his descent into the blackness of degeneration. Bäumer's now loosely structured 1917 military world begins to break down. The images of death and dying increase. The only distinction between men becomes whether they are living or dead, and Bäumer's comrades die more frequently, more variously, and more terribly (*AQ*, 229).

In the martial dance of death, Bäumer especially condemns army doctors. Bäumer describes the Catholic hospital where he is sent to recuperate in terms of bawdy high comedy and black humor. Doctors "get" a man under an operating knife, cripple him through amputation, and have a "glorious time" at it. In rooms with doors deliberately left open, nuns pray for sick soldiers, who only resent their prayers. Bäumer stops the prayers by throwing a bottle; he is never discovered as the culprit. From this diverting incident, which Remarque uses to shield the very serious business of prayers for the dying, there next follows the episode of a patient named Lewandowski hatching a plan to sleep with his wife in the hospital. The plan succeeds, with the cooperation of Lewandowski's comrades. (One wonders whether this incident was based on fact or fiction.) This episode and an earlier one in chapter 1 were excised by Little, Brown from the first U.S. edition of *All Quiet*. It is hard to imagine now any reader's moral objection to a scene, however startling, that Remarque handles with tactful and sensitive language and that illustrates young Bäumer's wise but pessimistic observation that in war men will live out their passions even as they are called to fight and die.

At the end of the novel Bäumer recovers and returns to the front. This return is clearly a death sentence. Stylistically, the language of meditative thought and introspection predominate, and the war's narrative becomes secondary. In 1918 (the last year of the Great War) the men of Bäumer's company either die off or are killed by the enemy's superior battle strategies and military equipment. Life and survival on the front—described impressionistically as an oily mass with yellow pools and spirals of blood (*AQ*, 241)—are as uncertain as rumors of peace. Time passes and "dissolves." Kat, Bäumer's closest comrade, falls one day as he returns from hunting for food. The last image of Kat is that of the prototypical father, providing food and thereby life. When Kat dies, Bäumer is prostrate and reels with fear over his solitude. As in classical tragedy, Bäumer is made to suffer the delusion of the "retarding moment," that is, the false hope that he can overcome his witness of so much suffering. Bäumer does not survive the Great War, however, and his anonymous death is Remarque's pessimistic answer to the proponents of war as a moral and patriotic source of individual rebirth.

# 7

# Characters and Characterization

A fiction writer reveals the *character* of imaginary persons, but when these imaginary persons seem lifelike to the reader they are said to have undergone *characterization*.[1] The reader experiences characterization in *All Quiet* through an aggregate of believable contexts and believable relationships between Remarque's characters. These relationships and contexts are either human or impersonal and are set either amid human beings or against a background of nonliving objects whose presence gives density to the physical world. This latter, secondary aspect of characterization in *All Quiet* will be discussed at the end of this chapter.

Human characterization in *All Quiet* logically holds the reader's primary interest. Remarque uses three levels of figures who stand out or recede into the landscape of the text: (1) the protagonist Bäumer, (2) a group of intermediate characters, and (3) a collection of sundry background figures. As Remarque's spokesman, Bäumer is the primary character through whom the author raises central issues in the novel and sets forth an increasingly penetrating perspective on the nature of war. The degree to which the reader experiences Bäumer as a rounded, three-dimensional character and a credible narrator influences, shapes, and guides his or her acceptance of authentic characterization in the novel. In other words, Remarque's ability to characterize well is reflected in the reader's acceptance of his characters as trustworthy spokespeople for the reality presented in the world of the novel, the world of the Great War. Although Remarque focuses on certain elements of Bäumer's characterization, Bäumer's fate nevertheless symbolizes more than the death of just one single German soldier. The reader's distance (the reader's nearness to or distance from the characters) also plays a key role in his or her belief in the honesty of Bäumer's character. Bäumer's role is not improbable in the wider context of war, and Remarque controls the reader's involvement with or detachment toward the characters, the reader's emotional and intellectual identity with them.

## INTERMEDIATE CHARACTERS

Intermediate-level characters serve a specific function in fiction, and their characterization is limited. Paraphrasing E. M. Forster's discussion of characterization in *Aspects of the Novel* (1927), intermediate characters are usually flat or one-dimensional and effectively disappear from a book once their purpose is served.[2] Kat is such an intermediate figure; an army veteran, he stands out as the classic soldier-representative of common sense and survival. He provides food for young recruits and, in fact, acts in loco parentis. Kat becomes Bäumer's best friend and confidant, as well as mentor, but he lacks Bäumer's philosophical depth and spiritual insight into war as a tragic modern experience. Consequently, the reader ranks Kat's role in the novel on a lower level than Bäumer's. Other intermediate characters are the teacher Kantorek and the postman Himmelstoss. Their stereotypically negative functions contrast with Kat's but are nevertheless important in lending credibility to Remarque's notion of a petty German (and European) bureaucratic and authoritarian world. With their conformist, exigent behavior, Kantorek and Himmelstoss are holdovers from the Wilhelmine social and military system. Bäumer's sanity as a soldier is exposed to the inherent banality of Kantorek's and Himmelstoss's warped understandings of war and German patriotism (*AQ*, 26–27).

If Kantorek and Himmelstoss stand out at one end of the intermediate character spectrum, Kat is at the other end, serving the function of being a touchstone by which we measure the pretensions and eccentricities of human behavior. Kat and Bäumer offer similar but different solutions to the blindness and folly of war. They suffer the same anonymous death on the battlefield, but Kat's simple and static characterization provides the reader with a point of reference from which to measure change and growth in Bäumer. Bäumer illustrates evolving insight into one's spiritual condition, and Remarque gives him a firm moral vision that seems to be lacking in Kat, thus limiting the expressive possibilities of Kat's ethical and symbolic function in the novel. Yet Kat can openly point up the protagonist's dilemma, and his traits are in many ways more representative of the human condition. Kat is a "transitional agent," a true intermediate-level character who, in providing simple thematic relief to the exceptional course of Bäumer's life, offers an effective example of common humanity that some readers will prefer to the more probing dilemmas and ambiguous issues posed by the novel.

## BACKGROUND CHARACTERS

A third kind of characterization is found in the miscellaneous figures who occupy the background of sundry settings, ranging from the noncombatant scenes to the fighting areas of the front. Soldiers eat their rations and read their mail. There are brief, singular encounters with French-speaking women. Bread is exchanged for sexual favors (*AQ*, 127). Worthy of mention are the Russian prisoners of war Bäumer meets, his fellow patients in the hospital, and the townspeople he encounters during a visit home. Remarque's background characters create the flotsam and jetsam of wartime humanity; without them, Bäumer's meditations on the futility of war would remain only abstract philosophical essays. The background characters help Bäumer establish his own reality vis-à-vis the mass (and ruins) of a society unhinged by the abnormality of war.

## THE PROTAGONIST

Understanding the elements of Bäumer's characterization, however, is crucial. Neither intermediate nor background characters are as essential as he to the central aesthetic and philosophical themes of time and identity, freedom and causality. These ideas define and regulate human experience in fiction and can contribute to truthful and convincing characterizations (Harvey, 100–149). Time in Remarque's novel is both subjective and historical. The connection between Bäumer's subjective sense of time and his personal growth is fundamental to his characterization. What the reader experiences as Bäumer's individuality is known finally against the background of changing periods of both chronological and subjective time. Bäumer's biography or personal history, like time itself, is both episodic and plastic.

In terms of historical time, Bäumer's identity was formed by his working-class origins and his role as a "victim" of a Prussian educational system with the hidden agenda of compelling submission to the cultural status quo. The adult Bäumer refuses to walk the thin line connecting renunciation of personality to unquestioning national loyalty. He tries to develop his own definition of heroism, one far removed from the party line of the German gymnasium and the German military. Bäumer's attempt to clarify historical and social time moves inevitably into the realm of his maturing identity and his concomitant questions about the meaning of lost time. As a protagonist under the influence of time, Bäumer's reflective sense can only note that the fiasco of his hollow education actually replicates the collapse of the emotional ties within his family circle. Both institutions—the school and the family—miscarry in the novel as regulators of social order in the German empire. Bäumer's father and his teachers share the same hope for a "breakthrough in Flanders" and in the German invasion of Paris (*AQ*, 144). At this point the discerning reader remembers that the kaiser's army failed to enter the French capital during the Great War.

Toward the end of the novel (in chapter 11) distinct time and identity diminish for Bäumer, and the reader's sense of time also undergoes a process of psychic decomposition. This breakdown process signifies the end of Bäumer's effort to maintain a distinction between his self and the outer world. This separation was always the difference for Bäumer between true identity and the commonplace. His identity, however, is marked less and less by a human context. A key sentence here is Bäumer's thought that now "they" are soldiers first, and "shamefaced" individual men second (*AQ*, 229). The flow of time at the novel's conclusion moves in the direction of death and the loss of both historical and subjective time. Bäumer's identity is lost in anonymity. This process denotes not only a personal loss but also the price exacted by time. As an individualized character, Bäumer stands out at the beginning of the text, but at the end his uniqueness is submerged into the mass of wartime devastation.

If Bäumer's character and characterization are affected by time, then categories of freedom and causality are also important in defining his character, both as an individual and as a soldier. What Bäumer can do is as important as what he cannot. Where is he limited and where is he a free agent? As a realistic novel, *All Quiet* initially tries to maintain a normative balance between Baumer's self and the outer world, a setting of relative freedom in which men usually live in the sense that they are "free" to make choices from many alternatives and that they learn to live with their choices. What actually happens in any work of fiction, however, is very different: as in *All Quiet*, the author chooses to tilt the balance in one direction. Especially at the end Bäumer becomes a deterministic figure, exposed by Remarque as a victim of a planned, political war. He dies from the undefined underlying causes of the Great War and their tragic, unresolvable consequences. This is classic determinism: the world is more important than the self.

Bäumer's background as a student of lower-class origins induced him to dream of a better life. His hope of social self-improvement— and his subsequent failure to achieve it, for reasons Bäumer himself cannot control—distinguishes him from other characters in the novel, including Kat, his best friend and comrade. Bäumer, as Remarque clearly shows, is finally profoundly aware of the freedom he has lost, and his fate corroborates the harsh assessment by social historians of Germany's ruling classes. Remarque knows and describes Bäumer's early social environment from his own experience. As a product of deterministic social forces, Bäumer never had the luxury of refusing entry into the German army as an enlisted man. He can only imagine doing a military tour as a noncommissioned officer. Other novels might show, in a realistic way, a protagonist's history of choices and the consequences of those choices, but the history of Bäumer's life really excludes those choices, thus conveying a sense of inevitability.

So as a protagonist Bäumer never represents an overt challenge to the German political and military system. It is rather Remarque's intention to show Bäumer as an individual being gradually confronted with the contradiction between his duty to his comrades, and to the war, and his penetrating insight into man's evil propensity for making that war. Bäumer is a very believable character in those passages in which the reader experiences him as a figure of deterministic social forces. But he is also most believable as a character in those passages in which the reader has access to thoughts and emotions that are clearly Bäumer's own, and in which it is obvious that he is beginning to think for himself. Such thoughts and sentiments are inner-directed and reveal the spiritual freedom he is acquiring. In the first chapter, for instance, we are drawn to Bäumer's astute observation that the world's unhappiness is "brought on by small men" (*AQ*, 15), and that plain and poor human beings have never started a war. Bäumer's subjective thoughts, however, are fundamentally subversive to any imposed system of law and order. The danger in his ideas lies in their being openly and audibly spoken. When "small" men acquire unnaturally great authority, they can become petty and vindictive. Bäumer's brief subjective experience—his foray into what can be called "subjective" freedom—provides a temporary break in the deterministic network of events that manages to subvert the system in a subtle and provocative way.

A similar lesson in smallness is found in chapter 9 in an episode about the "flying" visit of the kaiser to Bäumer's unit and the ceremonial awarding of Iron Crosses. In person, the kaiser seems smaller and less powerful to the men than the leader of legend. Bäumer himself is "rather disappointed" after seeing the great man. His friends even argue about how such a small man could have started a war. The kaiser's brief, dreamlike appearance on the field of battle obliquely and symbolically confirms the vanishing social and political world of 1914. The reader wonders whether Bäumer and his comrades grasp the portentous meaning of what would be the kaiser's last visit to the German front.

In the end, of course, Remarque's vision of freedom for Bäumer is close to Emile Zola's classic naturalist notion of resolute destiny: men's lives are controlled by the material forces of their environment. The "Summer of 1918" passages in the eleventh chapter blend daring, subjective outrage against war and examples of deterministic forces hard at work (*AQ*, 240). There will be no alternative to the physical collapse of the German fighting units; Remarque's metaphor of dying German soldiers turning into slaughtered animals is inescapable. As the animal-like gestures of human characters are described, human individualization, and the distinctive human context, are lost. With this turn toward dehumanization, Remarque seems no longer responsible for developing the personhood of his characters, not even Bäumer's. But Bäumer in the midst of deep physical despair becomes an abnormality, an externalized being with little will or volition. Elsewhere, shrapnel brings forth the cries of wounded soldiers and "shattered life" groans like dying animals. The hands of men are "earth," their bodies "clay," their eyes "pools of rain" (*AQ*, 242). Remarque abandons any pretense here at characterization within a human context, and at the tragic conclusion the horror of a useless war overcomes the reader. Like Bäumer and the author himself, the reader can no longer tell the difference between the dead, the wounded, and the survivors.

As readers of Remarque's novel, however, we are naturally concerned with the difference between Bäumer's characterization as a fictional human being and as a soldier from real life (Forster, 69). To what extent does Bäumer replicate the natural responses of any human being in similar circumstances? To what degree does Remarque play the role of a historian rather than that of a novelist preoccupied with characterization? To whom does everything happen? These final questions touch on Remarque's techniques of characterization. A historian deals with facts and with the ostensible activities of people in relation to those facts, but a novelist's chief business lies surely in examining the hidden life of his characters. It seems that, in *All Quiet*, Remarque is first a novelist and then, as a historian, the writer of a war novel. He never claimed to have written a history, but the record of Bäumer's activities as a common soldier—an identifiable German enlisted man going through his daily routine, within combat range on the western front, and finally getting killed—is a credible account of an actual wartime experience. That Remarque reveals the intricacies of Bäumer's *inner life* is another matter; doing so, he is a novelist creating a character. How far Remarque chooses to expand the figure of Bäumer is finally the reason he emerges as the protagonist.

As we have seen, Bäumer's character is well rounded while Kat's, Kantorek's, and Himmelstoss's are stereotypical. They are surface figures because certain key facts of character—birth, love, death—remain forever unexplored in them. Remarque points out that, if birth and death are the polarities of the mystery surrounding a man's life, then Bäumer's birth into a poor family was a determinant element in predicting his future. The mystery of Bäumer's character lies also, however, in having been born under a "dark star" whose blackness runs parallel to the deterministic flow of German social and political history. Remarque therefore emphasizes Bäumer's youth and the failed promise of his education. As the novel proceeds, the mysteries of Bäumer's character are gradually exposed for the reader's judgment and discernment. Bäumer's birth and death are related phases of the "hidden" life that Remarque, more as a novelist than as a historian, believes are extremely important in understanding the character of his protagonist. Bäumer's characterization thus shows us that a novelist, in creating characters, is free to choose or reject anything in composing the fictional life of his characters. Love, for example, appears in *All Quiet* as love for friends (comradeship) and country. Bäumer's love for Kat, engendered by war, is a noble human emotion that surely helps to define his character. And Bäumer's love for his country is a special kind of patriotism that never leaves him, even in his worst hour. The silence and inexpressability of that love is both altruistic and tragic.

Such a mixture of emotions in Bäumer's characterization leads the reader to understand the complexity and diversity of love.

Though we may never be able to say that Bäumer's authenticity as a character matches historical particularity, we leave the novel with the notion that a life like Bäumer's is explicable within the parameters that Remarque established. That those parameters are perhaps even "truer" than history may explain the long-lasting success with readers of the novel's characterizations.

Finally, characterization for Remarque's protagonist in *All Quiet* arises from a texture of relationships between Bäumer and nonliving objects. How this level of characterization works will interest the reader of the novel.

Concrete objects in Paul Bäumer's world are either life-saving or death-related. Those creative works associated with his early life—books, plays, and music (chapter 2)—are contrasted with those objects with which war has replaced them: grenades, shells, and machine guns. As a soldier, Bäumer's character must function amid concrete objects in an increasingly senseless universe. The objects of war, Remarque says, emphasize the contingency of a man's character and his life in wartime: war deforms the environment and makes men anonymous. The absurdist texture of objects in *All Quiet* works against the traditional separation between men and the primitive world of objects. The reader soon realizes that Bäumer's martial world is malign and sinister and works effectively against the conventional security and stability of things as signs of material wealth, as shown in the novels of Dickens and Tolstoy, early European practitioners of realistic fiction. In the works of these two novelists, objects (clothing, food, and furniture) are meant to sustain life and bourgeois prodigality. By contrast, whatever is lost in Bäumer's earlier civilian world—from the printed pages of German classical texts to the trees and grass of the Pappelgraben—is permanently irretrievable in the physical context of war. Whenever objects around him disappear, they are designated as mere "facts of mind or memory," rather than a condition of brute, simple facts that could bear witness to the concrete persistence of things, and thus shape character as they do for Dickens and Tolstoy. Here the discerning reader is reminded (in another context) of a character from Sartre's novel *La Nausée* (1938), Roquentin; while riding in a streetcar, Roquentin is overcome by a sense of living in the midst of nameless things. Bäumer, like Roquentin, is increasingly prey to the role of chance, a power that operates to expunge human control and direction over things. In Bäumer's war setting, things lose their names, merge into a state of flux, and become underlying elements of the faceless aspects of war. The reader's normal perception of character-thing relationships as stabilizing factors is thus reversed; this reversal is relevant to understanding alienation as a component of characterization in the novel.

# 8

# Adrift: Ending a Trilogy

Paul Bäumer's death on the western front was not Remarque's last word on the tragedy of the Great War, or even on the fate of the generation of German soldiers conscripted to fight it. He wrote two subsequent novels that, with *All Quiet*, make up a trilogy covering the war years and the immediate postwar period of German recovery efforts. *The Road Back* (1931) and *Three Comrades* (1937), however, are more than simply important sequels to Remarque's more famous first novel.[1] They continue his examination of the ethos of *Kriegskameradschaft*, that uniquely German sense of the spiritual bond between men when their lives are on the line during battle. In *Road* and *Comrades* Remarque shows how the aborning world of Weimar democracy neglected the returning German soldier. Remarque also felt that, as a writer, he could do narrative and thematic justice to the postwar themes of social and political disintegration. The dissolving of a homogeneous body of wartime survivors into crisis-driven civilians forms the narrative trajectory of *Road*; the story of their several lives is the basis of *Comrades*. This chapter will consider the thematic relationship to *All Quiet* of each of these works.

Remarque's German- and English-language publishers, predictably, had commercial reasons to press ahead with sequels to *All*

*Quiet.* Putnam's in London and Little, Brown in Boston were both aware that Remarque's name guaranteed continuous book sales and feature film commitments.[2] Otto Klement, Remarque's shrewd and knowledgeable literary agent, forthrightly defended Remarque's financial and legal interests as an international author. Klement's vital role in the early years of Remarque's celebrity is evident from the correspondence in Little, Brown's files. His guiding hand is also revealed in an October 1929 *New York Times* article in which the young author cites intrusions into his private life.[3] In the article Remarque carefully clothed in secrecy his creative plans, what he termed his withdrawal into the "unknown" to begin work on a successor novel to *All Quiet.* But he would prove that he could write a second major work. Remarque's expectation that he would write a book on Germany in the aftermath of the war was most probably due to the urging of Klement, who understood public sentiment and the desire of publishers to make a profit.

Remarque's chosen literary retreat was, not surprisingly, Osnabrück, his provincial birthplace in northern Germany. During the first of two trips to Osnabrück to write *The Road Back*, Remarque lived modestly in rented rooms he found through a newspaper advertisement. *Road* would reflect his strong personal and artistic dependency on a setting with which he was thoroughly familiar: Osnabrück in 1919–20, a time of cultural and political change. That year was especially turbulent for the nascent Weimar Republic. Remarque's school friend and first biographer, Hanns-Gerd Rabe—who appears in *Road* as Rahe (Rabe 1970, 227)—reminds both the reader and the critic that Remarque replicated many local places and people in *Road.* Only a later novel, *The Black Obelisk* (1956), contains a comparable number of local references and landmarks. In *Road* one can identify the city cathedral, the town hall, the marketplace, the *Hakenstrasse* (Haken Street), and a local river shaded by linden trees. The reader enters a domain that is sometimes alluded to, though only impressionistically, in *All Quiet. Road,* for example, sheds light on Remarque's earlier critique of the German teacher training system; the novel gives us a physical and material feeling for the buildings and classrooms of an educational system set in steel. *Road* is also a *Heimkehrer* (war returnee) novel, and one that is heavily dependent on the autobiographical link between its author and his birthplace. The postwar readjustment for the German veteran returning to a provincial city was inherently different from starting over in Munich or Berlin. Urban postwar readjustment would also be the topic of Remarque's third major novel, *Three Comrades*.

Remarque's practice was to first publish his novels in newspapers or periodicals. Such prepublication prepared the way for later hardback printings of the book. Otto Klement arranged simultaneous newspaper serialization of *Road* in prestigious European publications during December 1930: the *Vossische Zeitung* in Berlin, *Pester Lloyd* in Budapest, and *Le Matin* in Paris.[4] *Collier's* was chosen as the American outlet. The hardcover printing of the German edition of *Road* was announced on 30 April 1931 by the Ullstein media conglomerate, the original publisher of *All Quiet*. But *Road* was revised and corrected by Remarque up to the last minute. Arthur Wheen, Remarque's first English-language translator, was uniquely responsible for the success of this second translation project, which he received in batches from the author and his agent.[5] The finished novel was worth the long wait. It bore little indication that Remarque had incorporated incidents and episodes from several wartime stories and sketches and peacetime romances, published in *Collier's* from March to August 1930, about returned veterans who fail the test of civilian living.[6] It emerged from its last metamorphosis as a work of literary restraint and affective power.

## THE ROAD BACK

Remarque's second major novel is divided into seven parts, preceded by a prologue and followed by an epilogue. The prologue picks up the story of German Number Two Platoon somewhere in France about a week before the end of the Great War. Rumors are circulating that the kaiser has run across the border to Holland for safety. There are also signs that an armistice will be declared, but the time and place for a "farewell to arms" are both mysterious and almost unfathomable.

In the prologue Remarque introduces the men still surviving at this late date in the conflict: Ernst Birkholz, Remarque's central narrator and, like some of his comrades, a former student; his friends Ferdinand Kosole, Willy Homeyer, Heinrich Wessling, Albert Trosske, and Adolf Bethke; and Lt. Ludwig Breyer, a platoon commander and commissioned officer. Remarque has assembled a new cast of soldiers. The text makes only a cursory allusion to Paul Bäumer, Kat, and Müller, all of whom are lying somewhere "out there" on the battle lines of the front (*RB*, 20).

The men do not openly celebrate when peace finally arrives. Whom or what can they celebrate? As the survivors of the war finally leave for home, their relationship to what they are leaving behind becomes problematic. Ernst wonders whether the German defeat symbolizes "lost years" or "lost comrades" (*RB*, 21). At this early stage of the novel, it seems that wartime comradeship will survive as the healing power behind postwar social cohesion and survival. Ernst also seems prepared to give up his own selfish interest in the "lost years" of the war to the notion that the war was fought for defensible ideals.

The posing of such alternatives, however, is a sign from the author that *Road* will offer no easy solutions to the problem of postwar readjustment and the test of comradeship in a peacetime setting. An early reviewer noted perceptively that the soldier returnees' successful assimilation into German postwar life required that they first "escape" the wartime culture of the front, a culture with its own morals, hierarchy, and language.[7] Their experience in the Great War was necessarily focused on the manly cooperation between soldiers facing death. In four years a German soldier became a *Kamerad*, a member of a cult that effectively excluded German civilians. Both *All Quiet* and *Road* provide many examples of the civilian threat to the kind of order and stability that soldiers discovered for themselves while fighting the enemy and dreaming of a German postwar world. In peacetime Osnabrück and Weimar Germany, however, Remarque's returnees are threatened with extinction if they resist social pressures to adjust to conventional living conditions. They face opposition from civilian society and even the loss of their identity as comrades and survivors of the recent national crisis. Their no-win situation is the central thematic paradox of *Road*.

The "way back" is a twisted road across a no-man's-land into the trenches of peacetime living. Remarque's characters discover that a Weimar German civilian lives under a different code of morals and ethics. Among the physical and political signs of a society in transition is a lesser degree of tolerance for deviation from the peacetime-imposed rules of law and order. To settle their problems, the soldier returnees are obsessed by the desire to return to "symbolic" foxholes and dugouts, terrain with which they are familiar (Fadiman, 585). Their "enemy," however, is a peacetime German society that is scarcely unified in its political and social objectives. The returnees' struggle in *Road* is first of all an external struggle with changed and changing social and political forces, not with a specific and known enemy or other particular figures. Such an abstracted external conflict dilutes the continual efforts of Ernst Birkholz and his comrades to achieve self-vindication and restore personal identity. Personal internal conflicts in the novel increase the tension and the precarious status of life for all in the incipient democratic Weimar Republic.

Part 2 of *Road* introduces the complex details of the emerging social conflict. Ernst is soon brought forward as the protagonist in the traditional way: his point of view is revealed through the affecting trinity of action, thought, and feeling. At the Osnabrück railroad station, Ernst and his returning comrades meet up with a ragtag revolutionary soldiers' army (*RB*, 61). The enlisted men's soldiers' councils (*Räte*) mentioned at the conclusion of Ludwig Renn's novel (*War*) have come to pass. Ernst and his friends are thus challenged to show leftist solidarity when these Communist sympathizers demand that Lieutenant Breyer remove his officer's shoulder markings. Willy Homeyer laughs disdainfully at this hometown attempt to make a "bloody fine" revolution (*RB*, 65). If the world (German society) changes, it will be "his way," and he overtly refuses to take orders from a leftist group. Breyer is able to keep his stripes, and a leftist sergeant compromises by consenting to salute the man behind the uniform, not the uniform itself. The salute becomes a tribute to the memory of dead comrades in a capitalist war. This episode is an early signal that comradeship among the returnees will be challenged by the Left, that the word *comradeship* itself is changing in the wider context of Weimar peacetime life. The full impact of this initial episode, however, enters Ernst's consciousness only later in the novel. At this point, he is still too inner-directed and subjectively oriented to his recent past to even imagine the true parameters of his civilian readjustment.

Ernst is next seen in the protective environment of his home; this episode echoes the morbid tone of a similar episode in *All Quiet*, when Bäumer returns to his family on leave. Ernst (like Bäumer) resists assimiliation into the familiar setting of lower-class German culture, and he refuses to play the "child" before his adoring mother (*RB*, 68). A heavy curtain separates the life of the former schoolboy and that of the soldier returnee. His father craves stories about Ernst's wartime experiences with his comrades. Ernst is silent and wonders how to render his experiences conventionally enough that his father will understand them. Remarque's knowing narrative portrait of how a father and a son fail to communicate is a lesson in the miscommunication between two different generations. Remarque implies that the veterans have been stunned into silence by the horror of military combat, while the older Germans have learned the "art" of survival in civilian circumstances.

Though *Road* has a cast of diversified characters, the special destiny of Remarque's central narrator bears the thematic and narrative weight in a book that is clearly autobiographical in origin. Ernst (like Remarque) must resume and conclude an interrupted teacher training program (*RB*, 117)—predictably, the Catholic Teacher Training Seminar. The seminar tries to assert its former civil and moral authority over its former students. Part 2 concludes with a detailed description of the challenge these returning students pose to the conservative character of the imposing Prussian academic trainers and their curriculum. When the teachers and returned pupils meet, it is quickly revealed that there are fundamental differences between them over unfulfilled prewar academic requirements. Moreover, the veterans refuse to tolerate platitudes in a welcoming speech that compares their wartime heroism on the front to the "quieter" heroism of those who maintained the German civilian hearth (*RB*, 122). Their resistance challenges the sacred institutions of German education. But both sides are intractable. The brazen manner in which the veterans confront their principal and masters makes the reader cheer but portends disaster and failure for Ernst's career as a teacher. Ernst is doomed to have a short career as a social and cultural conformist under the iron heel of the educational bureaucrats.

The students refuse to play the role of "brave" scholars or even "good" schoolboys. They consider themselves returned "soldiers." At this point of the novel the men stand together as wartime comrades against the educational establishment, with Ludwig Breyer as their spokesman (at an initial convocation). At first this group makes the point that they all left civilian life with martial enthusiasm but returned alienated and disaffected. The German fatherland changed for them from a public symbol into a personal ideal, one no longer attached to meaningless rhetoric and fine phrases. The student returnees decide to stand together against the authorities. They petition the provincial and federal governments for less burdensome graduation requirements. (Remarque and a friend made such a trip to authorities in the provincial capital of Hannover, where concessions were made to the veterans [Rabe 1970, 218]).

Parts 4 and 5 relate how Ernst's comrades adjust to Weimar civilian life and confront postwar reconstruction as social outcasts. One becomes a smuggler, swapping Goethe ("a mile of culture") for "half an inch" of business. Another marries the daughter of the local butcher to ensure a supply of food on the table. The group makes a faint-hearted try at a regimental reunion. Georg Rahe, a disenchanted comrade, announces that readjustment to civilian life (marked by domestic order, duty, and women) has been a failure (*RB*, 214). Airy plans for a Sparticist (Communist) revolution collapse, and the comrades make a mad scramble instead for jobs and bourgeois security. Georg's solution is to return to a place where comradeship can still be found: briefly touring with the *Freikorps* (loosely assembled Weimar mercenaries), he makes a desperate return to the western front, where Remarque contrives to make him relive his past. Georg kills himself. An undeniable strain of morbidity begins to dominate the author's portrait of the returnees' lives in the small provincial city, contributing to a decided turn in reader expectations. The madness of war (*All Quiet*) and the unsettled normalcy of peace (*Road*) exchange places. Minds that were clear and united by Kriegskameradschaft on the western front fall into the delirium and hysteria of peace. Ludwig Breyer also kills himself, because he has syphilis. Max Weil, a friend of Ernst and an army returnee, is shot by his former commanding officer during a war veterans' protest march. Civilian workers on strike join the marchers. "Where is the Fatherland's gratitude?" can be read on the protesters' signs. "Shakers" (shell-shocked men) and veterans who were blinded make up one contingent. The republican *Reichswehr* stands watch to guard the civil interests of the federal government. Their leftist "comrades" make an appeal to these soldiers not to shoot at their "brothers." Ernst witnesses the carnage. Bullets spill blood on the pavement, and women are shot. In the darkened rooms of the Holländische Diele, a local restaurant, the leftist protest contingent has set up a hospital.

This narrative episode relates an important bit of Osnabrück's history and shows that the economic and social warfare in the unsettled postwar years of the Weimar Republic spread beyond Germany's major cities. For Ernst the bloodshed is devastating. Machine guns have "settled" the comradeship question in a definitive way: soldiers shooting at soldiers. For Ernst everything is "ended" when comradeship is killed. His presentiments are a harbinger of the emerging public resentment of the Weimar government, which was ridiculed by both the Left and the Right. The inability of the democratic regime then in place to establish political authority and civic order contributes to the underlying destabilizing forces in Remarque's novel. The primary need merely to stay alive in the social chaos supersedes the idealistic principle of comradeship among Ernst's friends.

When Ernst and his friend Willy pass their final examinations, they are offered their first teaching jobs in neighboring villages (*RB*, 222). Ernst believes that he is "fed up" with aimless drifting; brooding, melancholia, and introspection can now be replaced by a disciplined work ethic. Ernst is billeted at an old farmhouse and given 40 poor children for instruction. His school, a place where the pupils wear wooden shoes and a fire crackles in the stove, has three classes. This episode relating Ernst's "banishment" to a provincial *Volksschule* is based on Remarque's sad and contentious tenure as an elementary school teacher, as a substitute teacher at Lohne, a village within the sparsely settled Lingen district near the Dutch border.[8] A young appointee like Ernst was expected to be politically "clean" and establishment-oriented. *Road* relates in unadorned and factual detail the devastating impact of his gradual disenchantment with his teaching career.

Ernst's teaching interlude has the structure of a recurring nightmare. His wartime memories interfere with the rote nature of traditional instruction. Next to a crucifix (this is a public school governed by a Catholic priest) is a map of Europe. Ernst locates towns like Langemarck, Ypres, Bixchoote, and Stadten, the French and Belgian towns where the "big offensive" began on 31 July (*RB*, 225). A teacher and guide for the very young, however, cannot risk being distracted by the historical relevance of wartime events. The Great War is noticeably absent from his geography class. Ernst wonders whether he can teach his pupils about the fraudulent character of German learning, culture, and science. He calls himself a "bankrupt" man, one for whom the recent war destroyed every belief and almost every strength (*RB*, 252). Ernst (like Remarque) sees the hostility behind the community's superficial acceptance of him as a teacher. When he and a trainee colleague are challenged to a drinking bout in the village pub, he recognizes the invitation as a sign of contempt toward educated teacher probationers. Ernst's Sundays are almost intolerable: he sits in his room giving his imagination free rein to turn to visions of things past, including gray faces and cut limbs. His war memories become too much for him, and he loses faith in the viability of learning, culture, and science and in his ability to continue teaching. After experiencing mental depression and a subsequent breakdown, he decides to quit his job. The aftermath of the war has changed everything.

At Lohne the young Remarque underwent a tougher teaching regimen than does his fictional persona in *Road*, who quits his teaching post in the middle of his assignment and never returns. Remarque was charged with participating in the local Spartacist demonstrations. His political "activity" has been documented by Rabe in his researches on

Remarque's postwar teaching career (1970, 222). For this violation of civil service decorum, Remarque received a formal reprimand. On 4 May 1920 he moved to his next teaching assignment, a one-room schoolhouse in Klein-Berssen, Hummling, in the state of Prussia. Like the Lohne episode, Klein-Berssen, where Remarque challenged the authority of his Catholic supervisor, was an equally disastrous experience. There is every reason to believe that by the end of 1920 Remarque (like Ernst) had decided that he was not capable of continuing—or even wished to—as an elementary school teacher. It seems that Remarque, like the protagonist in his novel, failed to resolve the singular problems of postwar recovery and readjustment.

During a period of meditative introspection, Ernst comes to the valuable and timeless insight that his "road back" lies in achieving a "separate peace." His anger, bitterness, and disillusionment toward postwar German society are vented in the melodramatic courtroom trial of Albert Trosske, who is brought up on a murder charge. The wartime comrades try to argue a common plea for Trosske's innocence. The last war, they claim before the court, was the true murderer (*RB*, 327). That war taught soldiers to abandon the biblical distinction between life and death. The spilling of common blood on the battlefield swept away notions of patriotism, duty, and home. The comrades' final claim is that no civilian raised his hand to help the returning soldier. Their charge absolves or denies any personal moral responsibility.

The epilogue to Remarque's novel suggests a "rebirth" for Ernst in the manner of Goethe's Faust (*RB*, 335). A man (Ernst) is saved and brought up from the depths of existentialist despair. Ernst acknowledges that the "storm" that might have destroyed him has passed its intended "victim." If Faust, as a lasting symbol for man the overachiever, is saved by Goethe from suicide, then Remarque's simple veteran-protagonist learns an identical lesson—that nothing is ever lost, that dissension and alienation are never the last word. Ernst decides to devote himself to things that need to be built and repaired. The epilogue preaches stoically of "employment" for "feeble" hands and speaks of human beings with average powers. Like the Furies, the past (the Great War) will be excised from Ernst's memory. The book's conclusion suggests that a life-affirming personal catharsis will help him find his place. Remarque changes the consuming struggle for *Kriegskameradschaft* into the organic metaphor of life as the ferment and activity of growing cells rushing into the channels of a growing tree. This growth culminates in the green leaves that give the tree freedom. The author's solipsistic conclusion emphasizes the solitary nature of the road back to social and individual reintegration.

Remarque's sequel to *All Quiet* is no longer in print, and *Road* has suffered the onus of not being read. It has been overshadowed in German literary history by its more illustrious predecessor, though it was originally considered the author's indispensable last word on the German survivors of the Great War. *Road* sold at least 100,000 copies in the United States and was widely reviewed. *The Commonweal* especially praised Remarque's unique ability to "describe . . . (that) kind of thought and feeling which was . . . the only vital spiritual product of the conflict."[9]  The *Atlantic Monthly* called attention to the vitiated spirit running through the book and cited its artistic structure—Remarque's ability to manipulate his story as a series of incidents when he had "no plot of a conventional kind."[10]  The American film version of *The Road Back*, made by Universal Studios, was released in June 1937; today it is almost inaccessible.[11]  Six years went by before Universal dared to offer an initial (first) script to the German consul in Los Angeles, who threatened to boycott the film if the script's "fascist" ending (a group of student *Wandervögel* [scouters]) were not altered. The ending was altered by the studio before the film was shot. Even in the United States Remarque could not escape being politically controversial to both the extreme Right and the antagonistic Left.

And plenty of critical voices were ready to state an opinion on the passive, noncombative stance of Remarque's prose hero Ernst Birkholz. Otto Biha's lengthy review in the leftist journal *Literature of the World Revolution* laid out some basic reasons *Road* (like *All Quiet*) could never be "acceptable" to the international Communist party.[12] Biha criticized Remarque's first two major books for their failure to abandon fainthearted social abstractions and generalities and for their fetishist cult of "comradeship," for idealizing combat trench life. Remarque, said Biha, gave up progressive leftist ideology for musing, dreaming, and philosophizing. *Road* fails to "acknowledge" the proletarian standard-bearers of the revolution in the postwar Weimar government. Biha refused to believe that "front comradeship" could contribute to solving the real problems of a German society in need of being changed. Biha regarded Ernst's teaching fiasco as typical for a man (and author) who has no ideology or even reformist program. Biha also wondered why Ernst's final despairing and resigned tone is tendered under the cover of superficial, optimistic sentiment. Biha proclaimed that the novel's forced ending was a business requirement of the capitalist democratic press. The book's characters and their problems are "individualistically posed. . . . Petty-bourgeois egotism presumes to delineate the tragedy of mass suffering and mass privations" (Biha, 147).

## THREE COMRADES

Six years would pass before Remarque published *Three Comrades*, the last novel in his tripartite literary and autobiographical study of the Great War. In *All Quiet*, Remarque wrote about his generation during the trial of combat. *Road* presents the "failure" of that generation's adjustment to Weimar peacetime society. *Comrades* is about three specific men of that generation and their effort to cut through postwar cynicism and disillusionment. The third book of Remarque's war trilogy offers more than a simple reworking of themes in *Road*. Remarque not only sustains his creative powers of characterization in *Comrades* but revitalizes the popular genre of the romantic novel. Thematically, *Comrades* is similar to Ernest Hemingway's *Farewell to Arms* (1929), a romance set during the Great War. And like Hemingway's *The Sun Also Rises* (1926), *Comrades* is also a novel about a lost generation in that some of its characters who are survivors of the war have been rendered unfit for the structures of everyday life. In *Comrades* Remarque recasts familiar literary themes.[13]

The third book of the trilogy also proved that Remarque could refocus his creativity in a different direction. His early financial and personal independence had seductively opened up to him a lifestyle of luxury and cultural freedom that threatened his commitment to art and to pursuing a writer's career. Remarque's leftist critics fully believed that he had abandoned them in their continuing battles with the Weimar centrist government and the coming struggle for economic and political change. Remarque did not support the controversial status of Socialist or Communist parties. In 1931 he decided to buy a vacation retreat house on Lago Maggiore in Ticino, Porto Ronco, Switzerland, a historic villa once owned by the Swiss painter Arnold Böcklin; it provided a proper setting for Remarque's French impressionist paintings. He had begun to purchase art for practical reasons: he needed a way to direct his income away from the scrutiny of the German government. In 1932 Remarque's account in the German Darmstädter and National Bank (DANAT) was seized by banking authorities and he was charged with currency violations.[14] He subsequently made the prudent decision to spend part of the year in Switzerland where, as it turned out, he joined a growing permanent colony of other European and German artists and writers.

This period after the financial success of *All Quiet* and *Road* was assuredly one of consolidation during which Remarque set the future pattern of his literary career. He had made his way out of a lower-class provincial life into the vibrant culture of Berlin where, with proverbial beginner's luck, his first major book had brought him critical fame and economic security. Now he chose to live in Switzerland. To Remarque there was never any question of continuing to pursue a literary career. He did, however, make a definite decision to live and write on his own terms and conditions.

His desire at this time to free himself from the control of his publishers is evident in his correspondence with Little, Brown over contractual obligations for *Comrades*. In the fall of 1932 Remarque was in Ticino, Porto Ronco finishing his new book. In 1933 and 1934 Little, Brown was still asking about the status of the work, and it was not until December 1936 that Remarque finally finished *Comrades*. Blunt and bitter words were exchanged between Remarque and Little, Brown over the long delay in delivering the manuscript.

Remarque reminded Alfred McIntyre, then president of Little, Brown, that completing *Comrades* had cost him blood and nerves, but

McIntyre's response was equally to the point, namely, that as a businessman he would never again advance so much money for a book that had taken so long to complete.[15] Both men held their ground, neither one acknowledging the fundamental reasons for the delay in manuscript delivery and publication: history and politics. In January 1933 the advent of German National Socialism made Adolph Hitler the German chancellor. Now persona non grata in his homeland, Remarque was compelled to give up any idea of returning to Germany. On 10 May 1933 both *All Quiet* and *Road* were publicly burned by students and Nazi functionaries before the Berlin Opera House. Along with the works of other banned writers and intellectuals, Remarque's books could no longer be sold in German libraries and bookstores. It was not the first time Remarque's books had been burned or censored in Germany, but now he was cut off from his natural readers. His best alternative was to leave Germany and settle permanently in Switzerland, where he could await further social and political developments. Remarque became a literary exile in Switzerland, a "guest" of the Swiss government. He and Jutta Ilse Zambona, his divorced wife with whom he had only recently been reconciled but had not remarried, were allowed to live in Switzerland as long as they retained German citizenship.[16] It was under these traumatic and divisive circumstances that Remarque wrote, revised, and finished *Comrades*. The German-language edition was published in 1937 in Holland under the imprint of Querido Verlag, an Amersterdam publishing house that specialized in proscribed German exile writers. Remarque, however, could not rely on this unstable arrangement in a country that would soon become a target for Nazi occupation.

The time of *Comrades* is 1928, and the setting is primarily Weimar Berlin, but some of the narrative takes place in a mountain sanatorium. The "three comrades" are former soldiers whose lives were all interrupted by the First World War. One of the comrades is the chief narrator of the novel, Robert "Robby" Lohkamp. With his two friends—Gottfried Lenz ("the last Romantic") and Otto Köster—he runs a car repair shop, which provides them with only a grubby existence on the fringes of economic security. They rely on one another for emotional and brotherly support; their special ability to nurture each other derives from the spiritual comradeship they developed during the Great War. Otto owns the shop. He treats Lenz as an equal, despite Lenz's several years of drifting in South America. Robby's role in the novel is the most engaging. At first he seems cast from a fictional ancestry of antiheros, from the fashionable lineage of French and American novels. Robby is alienated, divided, and dehumanized by psychological and cultural determinism. Life in postwar Weimar Germany is not as he would want it, but he resolves not to spend his days engaged in self-pity.

When the novel opens, Robby is about to celebrate his thirtieth birthday. He agrees with Lenz and Köster that introspective sentiment on such a day is to be avoided. An alternative celebration is suggested: a drive into the country in "Karl," the pride of the repair shop. As a car, Karl is a physical presence in Remarque's novel and, on this birthday excursion, the means through which Robby meets Patricia "Pat" Hollmann, with whom he secretly falls in love (*TC*, 14). Meeting Pat signals a change in Robby's perception of himself and his surrounding world, a change depicted as a subtle process of increasing consciousness, both internal and external. Remarque's sensitivity to the theme of romantic love raises his protagonist out of the mundane and depressing environment of the boardinghouse where he lives. Robby's fellow tenants are castoffs of the deteriorating Weimar social order, especially Hasse, a pitiful clerk who works overtime in the fear of losing his job and his wife (*TC*, 24). Hasse is a symbol of stress-related violence and human cruelty that surface in times of attrition. Robby's second home is the International Café, the meeting place of his comrades and sundry prostitute friends.

"The day of great dreams is past," Robby muses at one point, although to the reader Remarque's antihero seems too young for such despondency (*TC*, 60). His remark is self-indulgent, however, the remnant of an introspective structure he has erected against the exterior world. A friend has told him that he is well off because he is "alone." But to be alone, Robby discovers, is to be at one's neediest and most vulnerable. In setting up his central character for a relationship with Pat, Remarque turns Robby away from his divided, alienated self and the cult of antiselfhood, indicating that his affair with her will be more than a casual relationship. Their relationship becomes an expression of faith in the viability of another human being, and in this sense *Comrades* can be read equally well as an existentialist text, based on Remarque's understanding of the *popular* version of that philosophy. In a German postwar world of "absurd" freedom, Robby's anxiety can be replaced by inner values. Pat Hollmann's love for Robby becomes a right choice in the midst of everyday absurdity and its dehumanizing pressures.

Köster, Lenz, and Robby were comrades together in the Great War, and now they are together in the car repair business. As Robby's mistress, Pat becomes a fourth comrade joining the trio, and here the novelist must show how love between a man and a woman conditions the course and definition of friendship among men. Gradually Pat is drawn into the group by virtue of her anonymity and free-heartedness, her ability to integrate into a "masculine" world—that uncharted terrain of male bonding that is ultimately revealed to be the story of four inconsequential people adrift in the vortex of the "back street of Berlin."[17]

Only gradually does Robby learn something about Pat's past life, especially about her preference for living alone and her apparent leaning toward older, richer men. Robby is a younger man who lives on "short credits," and he would normally distrust an independent woman. In the opening stages of his relationship with Pat, Robby is clearly a product of conventional mores and a postwar Weimar neurosis: the fear of "loss." When he refuses to permit Pat to sit for a painter friend, he sees such an act both as a means of seduction and the loss of love; the painter, on the other hand, levels the charge that there is a "generation's difference" between the two men (*TC*, 127). Such a commonplace phrase summons up deep emotions for the reader. But the story of Robby's relationship with Pat moves on many other levels. Remarque refuses to allow his alienated young narrator an easy entry into a neat romance. The immensity of Robby's inner changes are signaled by the author's attention to the smallest details. One evening the lovers decide to sleep with each other, and Robby is ashamed of his plain room. Pat stops in front of a wardrobe covered with colorful travel labels. Robby lies to Pat about his supposed trips to South America. In a remarkable and insightful moment of candor, Robby admits to himself that he had heard "it all" from Lenz, that "memory" and "desire" had mixed deliberately to add "glamour" to his hitherto "petty" and "obscure" life (*TC*, 135). Robby clearly fears that he will lose Pat's incredibly lovely face, which symbolizes hope and a chance for something better in his life. He also tells himself, however, that he is much too "little" to deserve whatever Pat might do for him as a comrade and a lover.

Meanwhile, the three comrades manage to sell a repaired Cadillac and buy a taxi with which they hope to make more money. Robby takes Pat on a seaside vacation, but it becomes clear that she is a sick woman. A day on the beach is an occasion for reverie and meditation (*TC*, 229). Robby remembers a summer interlude in 1917, when he and his soldier friends were granted a few days' holiday to leave Flanders and go to the shore at Ostend. Involuntary memory fills in the details of this bygone episode during the last war, perhaps a deliberate act of forgetfulness. The past excursion to the sea (like the current one with Pat) was actually a foreshadowing of approaching death, a moment spent in an illusion of freedom before his comrades Meyer, Holfthoff, and Lutgens died on the front. When Pat suffers a hemorrhage, her sudden sickness seems to repeat Robby's bloodstained past. He begins to rely heavily on Köster and Lenz, who drive him with Pat to Berlin, where she can recuperate and follow a doctor's regimen. A date is set for her return to a mountain sanatorium. The catastrophe impels Robby to scrutinize his relationship with Pat, and he sees that it has become a central fact of his life.

The idyll of friendship does not last long, however, and the fortunes of all the characters in the novel undergo a shift toward material and emotional deprivation. Hasse, the belabored boardinghouse tenant and harassed husband, lays out his bankbook and two letters (in proper order) and then hangs himself. His suicide bears out the truism that "a German never apologizes" but fatalistically submits to his bad luck (*TC*, 344–47). The three comrades' garage business slides precipitously toward bankruptcy. Contagious pessimism rules these Weimar lives as they move toward social and human deterioration.

Chapter 24 introduces into the narrative the themes of Weimar political tension and conflict. Lenz, until now a secondary character, is revealed to be a potential follower of mass politics. Remarque makes general references to the rising number of protest demonstrations and marches, but their particular identity is never in doubt. Besides the fascists' "military marches," Weimar leftists are also parading to the tune of the "Internationale" and the Berlin unemployed are demonstrating for work and bread. Strikers clash with the Berlin police. (These episodes recall similar incidents from *Road*, in which social unrest occurs in a smaller city.) One day Köster and Robby set out to look for the "missing" Lenz, who is probably at a political gathering. The two comrades visit three different meeting places and hear a different provocative message at each of them. Robby disdains the street rhetoric of a self-proclaimed "savior" of the poor and his "truths" of common venue: overall misery, starvation, and unemployment. His promises of utopian socialist reform, if elected, seem too good to be true. For Robby this appeal is fraudulent: in the reformist "lottery," every player only seems to be a winner. No one political party is the panacea for the country's problems. Robby and Köster hear the same message at the second political meeting, delivered this time amid banners and uniforms by an official, presumably the head of a conservative party, who speaks *Hochdeutsch* (Standard German). Köster and Robby find Lenz eventually in a tenement assembly room, hidden in a working-class district. Once again Robby, as Remarque's mouthpiece, is skeptical of the leftists' ability to save the Weimar government from political and economic collapse. While "surveying" the gathering, Robby says that the poor do not seek reformist politics but rather a "substitute religion" (*TC*, 402).

Remarque's cynicism toward and general condemnation of Weimar political affairs in *Comrades* once again brought down the wrath of leftist reviewers. F. C. Weiskopf called *Comrades* a *Roman im Niemandsland* (novel in nobody's land), noting that Remarque's three comrades live on a social "island" isolated from reality.[18] Weiskopf also claimed that the actual classes of Weimar society—the workers, the bourgeoisie, small shopkeepers, Nazis, Social Democrats, and Communists—are all invisible in Remarque's fictitious world. It is surprising, according to Weiskopf, that Lenz is shot by fascist street thugs, but Remarque does not seem to care whether the killers are common attackers or prototypes of the fascist bullies of the future. Remarque might have called Lenz's murder a political murder, but he does not, and the murder fades (according to Weiskopf) into the gauzy structure of Remarque's unbelievable Weimar political context. Not so surprisingly then, Weimar German leftists rejected *Comrades* as they had rejected *Road* and *All Quiet*.

A telegram comes for Robby to visit Pat in her mountain sanatorium, a setting all too reminiscent of Thomas Mann's novel *The Magic Mountain* (1924). The mountain episodes remind the reader that *Comrades* is also a poignant romance, even if they cannot be compared with Mann's powerful philosophical meditations on sickness and health, tragedy and humor. Remarque has neither the philosophical depth nor the desire to solve for Robby the "mystery" of Pat's death from tuberculosis. Robby's words at the end sum up his layman's response to her passing: "The details are wonderful, but the whole makes no sense," and, "A madman made the world on an idle day" (*TC*, 471). There is no accounting for the creation of the world or even man's happiness. Now both Pat and his work will disappear from Robby's life. Köster's shop is soon placed on the auction block. Remarque, whose "disoriented" perception of Weimar political and social reform was much criticized by the German Left, chooses instead to make the individual living in that culture responsible for his own destiny. Running like a red thread through Remarque's wartime trilogy is the word *comradeship*, which the author never ceases to offer as the humane alternative to the problems and dilemmas found in the texts.

With the dark conclusion of the last book in Remarque's trilogy, however, his central theme of comradeship as a viable alternative to negativity and postwar alienation had run its course and the reader apprehends what the author has wrought: a final definition of comradeship as a universal but ultimately pessimistic experience. Comradeship was the common inheritance of Remarque's wartime generation. *All Quiet* and *Road* stress both the singularity and commonality of that generation's shared insights into the human condition because of the Great War. *Comrades* extends the period and scope of Remarque's solitary inquiry into that shared destiny even further, from the time of early peace into the lingering reality of Weimar social chaos and the threat of new political instability. *Comrades* upholds comradeship initially as a nurturing act that defines oneself and one's mates as a protecting, common front (*Verteidigunsgemeinschaft*) against the wasteland of a satiated and exhausted postwar society. As sharers of an ominous destiny, Remarque's hard core of wartime survivors now comprises only a few hardy warriors. Ernst Birkholz in *Road* speaks of his future as a "road of toil . . . where he will be alone" (*TC*, 343). Robby Lohkamp is made silent and inarticulate by Pat's death. This silence is symbolically the end, the resting place, of a German generation overcome by a lingering anomie, a persistent alienation born of cultural and social decay. The road back from the western front confirms Remarque's tragic narrative insight into the imminent collapse of those German institutions that, like the fragile nature of comradeship, would fall under the weight of time and of ruthless political and historical cruelty.

# A WIDER CONTEXT

# 9

# Déjà Vu: Exile and After

Early on, the Nazi regime tried to entice the German non-Jewish writers living in the exile communities of Switzerland and Austria—even the coast of southern France—to return "home" and submit to fascist standards of art and literature. Then these German exiles were threatened with the loss of their German citizenship. Remarque himself was made subject to a July 1933 denaturalization and expatriation law. When his German citizenship was revoked on 4 July 1938 (Firda 1988, 103), no guarantee remained that he could live undisturbed, in the event of a new war in Europe, under the protection of neutral Switzerland. Owning property in Switzerland now became problematic. Remarque came to America, arriving in New York in March 1939 with Otto Klement, his literary agent, at his side.

The reinvigorated writer turned to a study of the evolving European exile problem and its accompanying social alienation. Remarque's novels *Flotsam* (1941) and *Arch of Triumph* (1946) are set in the disaffected orbit of forced exile and displacement. Remarque now believed that the forthcoming martial conflict of World War II was only the latest level of war as a permanent feature of European cultural displacement. *Flotsam* presents the topical exile issue of the bureaucratic nightmare of papers and passports for European exiles moving continually among Vienna, Prague, Zürich, and Paris. Legal "rights" of asylum float and shift metaphorically in the novel's maze of separate refugee stories that establish mood and atmosphere rather than sustained characterization. Remarque's narrative emphasis in *Flotsam* is on the adventure and even the melodrama of the exile experience. The sustained characterization we miss in *Flotsam* can be found in *Arch of Triumph*, whose protagonist is Ravic, an exiled German physician living in Paris just before the Nazi occupation. Ravic offers a rounded portrait of an introverted exile professional willing to do almost "anything" to escape the Gestapo. His seasoned cultural pessimism on the eve of World War II contains more than a reflection of Remarque's disdain for political events in Germany and his assessment of the country's future. Ravic and the protagonists of Remarque's earlier Great War trilogy are spiritual brothers. Like Ernst Birkholz and Paul Bäumer, Ravic is a Remarque antihero, vulnerable and doubtful that he can "escape" a world out of control.

*Arch* is a competent and above-average novel, incorporating cultural themes and philosophical issues that link it to its worthy predecessors in the Great War trilogy. Charles Poor noted in 1946 that Ravic is an existentialist, an uprooted individual who is ultimately thrown back on his own resources for survival and suffers a real loss of personal as well as ethnic and political identity.[1] As such, Ravic is a European *deraciné*, an addition to Remarque's arsenal of character types living out of concord with their time and place. Ravic's characterization was praised in favorable reviews of the novel, which was first published in the United States.

But caveats were delivered in some literary quarters when the narrative content of Remarque's novels shifted as a result of changes in the political environment. In 1968, for example, the critic Axel Silenius asked whether after *All Quiet* and *Road* Remarque had not lost his vital connection with the details and firsthand experiences of German life.[2] *All Quiet* and *Road* are unmistakably grounded in the writer's own German story; personal events and incidents flow convincingly and realistically into fiction. Silenius's point was that the longer Remarque stayed out of physical and cultural contact with German life, the more he was forced to rely on memory and hearsay, on secondhand documentation. This was, however, an unfair analysis of Remarque's evolution as an artist and writer. His literary strategies as an exiled writer and cultural spokesman were bound to change. Remarque could not remain only the writer of a famous first novel, or a writer with only postwar Weimar recovery as his subject.

In American exile he wisely refrained from returning to his original prototype as a spokesman for the lost German generation of the 1920s. In America the well-recognized author of *All Quiet* became a revered spokesman for German democracy, and he anticipated a liberated Europe. But with the publication in Europe of *A Time to Love and a Time to Die* (1954), a controversy arose that made the new book problematic for Remarque's post–World War II German public.[3] *Time*'s protagonist is Ernst Graeber, a Paul Bäumer double. World War II fascism and the German war on the eastern front provide the catalyst in this book for the evolution of the protagonist's higher self. *Time* is cast as a philosophical struggle between humane and evil principles. The town of Werden (Remarque's Osnabrück) is living under fascism. Graeber, like Paul Bäumer, is an everyman, but his early disillusionment with the German army comes from his country's program of racial and ethnic cleansing in a sullen, scorched-earth landscape. Remarque gives his antihero a love affair, making this war novel a popular wartime romance in which love becomes a regenerative symbol for Graeber. *Time*, like *All Quiet*, probes the question of the dubious survival of humanistic values in German society. German teachers are again a favorite Remarque topic. After visiting Pohlman, a former instructor, Graeber goes away indifferent to Pohlman's rationalized, academic explanation that no tyranny, even the Nazi one, can hope to endure. Graeber, like Paul Bäumer, gets no satisfactory answers to troubling questions. In *Time* earlier German history seems to be dolefully repeating itself. Graeber and his lover, Elizabeth, marry before he returns to the front. During a suspenseful episode when he is "ordered" to shoot four Russian guerrillas, Graeber moves to kill his commanding officer. Graeber himself is shot by one of the "free" Russians, who still consider him their enemy. This is a cynical ending to a novel in which the narrator argues that compassion and kindness are the antidotes to war.

Contrasting Paul Bäumer's death with Graeber's, the reader can perceive that not only do Remarque's young soldiers die under different circumstances but Graeber's death, unlike Bäumer's, occurs in a context of moral purification. Bäumer does not die in a direct act of rebellion against the Great War; there is reason to believe, however, that Graeber's accidental and tragic death occurs within the ample context of rejected fascism. Before he dies, Graeber is convinced that the war is wrong, and he moves to save a few human beings. Graeber's role as a symbol of resistance is finally openly demonstrable, a contrast to that of Bäumer's affecting passivity. Graeber's role is one of classic catharsis, and he embodies Remarque's wish that humaneness would survive in the German postwar civilian populace. There is no question that in *Time* Remarque broadened his critique of war beyond the questions posed by *All Quiet* and that he grappled with the sensitive question of Germany's collective moral burden as the instigator of the Second World War. Graeber is Remarque's bearer and expiator of such an inheritance of guilt and culpability. His tragic death seems to pay the "price" demanded by Remarque for the Nazi "nightmare." Graeber could never be considered a victim, or even the antihero of a lost generation, in the sense that Paul Bäumer is in *All Quiet*. In *Time* Remarque offers Graeber's death as a positive instance of his writer's faith that German life and history would renew itself. Without this wider framework of moral regeneration, Graeber's death on the eastern front would surely resemble Paul Bäumer's earlier on the western front in being no more than an anonymous event in the flow of history.

Publication of *Time* in Germany immersed Remarque in a new controversy: the German press discovered excisions from the German-language edition (Firda 1988, 72; Weiskopf, 254). *Der Spiegel* and *Die Welt* charged that Remarque's German publisher, the respected firm Kiepenheuer and Witsch, deleted the author's direct and indirect references to the SS character Steinbrenner and the suspected half-Jewish soldier Hirschland. There was no doubt that editions of *Time* published in other European countries were full and complete. German sensibilities, however, seemed to have been spared by the German publisher, which left out of Remarque's latest book the particulars of a war that had ended as another defeat over ten years before. While Kiepenheuer and Witsch did not deny making the deletions, it claimed that Remarque had agreed to publish in Germany a version of the book different from what was published elsewhere. The unanswered question remained: why had the German publisher been overly zealous in protecting German sensibilities about the country's culpability in the recent conflict? On the other hand, it could be argued that Remarque was hardly qualified to call his country to account. He had had no firsthand experience of life in Germany or in the army under the fascist terror. His account of Graeber's suffering as an enlisted man on the eastern front and his impressive resolution of the intense moral strife he depicts were strictly artistic: Remarque could never claim more than secondhand knowledge of these experiences. The fact that he had been safe in America during the Nazi regime gave many Germans yet another reason to question his sincerity and his compassion for those trapped in Germany who were denied free civil and artistic expression. Remarque tried to answer these charges—some of them justified—but he remained as distant as ever from the German political scene. The players in this reprise of the earlier 1929 political contretemps around Remarque showed the intensity, bitterness, and resilience of social memory. Remarque had dared to once again "insult" German military and ethnic dignity. As a perennial outsider who had left his country to live abroad, he was deemed ill equipped to engage in German consciousness-raising.

But as Harley Taylor points out, *Time* as a work of fiction is not only a "partial return" for Remarque to the formulaic structure of *All Quiet*, but a love story—an unbeatable combination, according to the American press and the Book-of-the-Month Club, whose huge printing of Remarque's World War II novel was a commercial success (195). American readers were sympathetic to a wartime romance about love among the "ruins" by a bona fide "survivor" of German fascist tyranny. They were unconcerned that *Time* was not a factual documentary about a liberal German soldier or a closet anti-Hitler revolutionary.

By the late 1950s Remarque's writing had indeed shifted in a different direction from that of the 1920s. Exile, the Second World War, and expatriation had confirmed his insights: German politics and social dissension had scarcely changed, and he would forever be a stranger to modern sensibility and morality. Remarque had moved finally into the grand theme of his artistic maturity: the condition of twentieth-century man was to be subject to the onslaught of cultural and social alienation. In retrospect, each of his novels, from *All Quiet* to the posthumous exile novel *Shadows in Paradise* (1971) (a roman à clef set in New York during World War II) seems to have been a part of his literary account of this deculturization process—the mass displacement of human beings caught in unjust wars, economic crises, and the symbolic crossing of national and ethnic boundaries. In this sense, *All Quiet*, his first novel that affected the hearts and moral sensibilities of readers everywhere, not only achieved a place in the history of German war literature but also had a starring role in his fictional reconstruction of his own life and times. The enduring popularity of all Remarque's novels attests not only to their readability but to their status as German and European cultural commentaries.

When Remarque died as a naturalized American citizen in a Swiss hospital on 25 September 1970, Hans Habe, a writer and a close friend of Remarque's in Switzerland, noted that no government representative from Germany, the United States, or even Switzerland attended the author's burial.[4] Not surprisingly, government bureaucracy was thus consistent in its desire to remain above the fray. The West German authorities never restored the German citizenship taken away from Remarque by the Nazis in the 1930s, but the author also refused to apply for such restitution. Some of Remarque's friends, however, obtained public recognition in Germany of his national and international stature. In 1963 Remarque was awarded the Justus Möser Medal by his hometown of Osnabrück at a ceremony in Ascona, Switzerland. Osnabrück thus recorded its appreciation for Remarque's "loving" remembrance of his birthplace. In 1967 the West German government took its turn at belated state recognition by awarding Remarque the Distinguished Service Cross of the Order of Merit of the Federal Republic of Germany (*Das Grosse*

*Verdienstkreuz*). Finally, Remarque was elected into the distinguished German Academy for Language and Literature. Each of these awards was a worthy recognition of Remarque's service to the cause of contemporary German literature and culture.

# 10

## Film Classic: The Film Adaptation of *All Quiet on the Western Front*

Any study of *All Quiet* must also consider that work's place in the history of notable literature adaptation into motion picture. In 1930 *All Quiet on the Western Front* was released as a Hollywood feature film, and from that time on Remarque's name would always be linked to Hollywood.[1] At least six later Remarque novels were chosen for feature film adaptation (Taylor, 1989). Remarque lived in Hollywood and New York during World War II, and, in fact, his literary career ran parallel to Hollywood's golden age of filmmaking in the 1940s and 1950s, a period when a close connection existed between literature and film adaptation. He supervised and negotiated contracts for film projects like *Arch of Triumph* (United Artists, 1948), starring Charles Boyer in the role of Ravic, and *A Time to Love and a Time to Die* (Universal-International, 1958), featuring John Gavin in the role of a German soldier disillusioned with service in Hitler's army. Remarque even married a film star, Paulette Goddard, who became his second wife after he divorced Jutta Zambona in 1957.

Hollywood moguls discerned the filmic aspects of Remarque's novels, the gestic quality of his literary style. Remarque may have written like a talented novelist, but he also had the special aesthetic vision of a writer of film scenarios. In his unique talent for constructing novels with episodic narratives—so amenable to film adaptation—Remarque followed the artistic tradition of novelists like the American William Faulkner, who did a stint in Hollywood, and F. Scott Fitzgerald, who worked on the MGM film adaptation of Remarque's *Three Comrades*.[2] His film work, however, seriously compromised Remarque's place in modern German literature in the eyes of those literary critics who scorned the idea of any artistic compromise between the writing of novels and the making of motion pictures. Correspondence between Remarque and Little, Brown clearly shows that the writer relished not only a hard business settlement but the prospect of Hollywood fame and fortune.

The film version of *All Quiet* was produced by Universal Studios under the leadership of Carl Laemmle, Jr., the son of Carl Laemmle, at a time when the older man, one of the original group of European Jewish immigrants who literally founded Hollywood, was ready to hand over his studio to his son. Carl Jr. announced a "drastic" change in studio policy: the studio would shift away from silent family entertainment toward big-budget sound features with challenging themes.[3] In 1929 the best-seller status of Remarque's novel, along with a revival of public interest in the Great War, induced Laemmle's son to buy the film rights to *All Quiet*. The war film, like the western, was a genre that had always found an audience, so studio production approval was never a problem for a director advancing a war film project. *Front* was conceived as a sound war genre film with pacifist overtones, but as the film historian Ivan Butler suggests, it was hardly a "courageous" production, for several reasons that will be discussed below.[4] That *Front* became a famous war film is a happy accident of film history. It remains a unique instance of the possibility of achieving both artistic and commercial success within the Hollywood studio system.

Carl Laemmle and his son went to Berlin in August 1929 to confer with Remarque on the film scenario for *Front*.[5] They hoped to secure the novelist's "cooperation," but their transcontinental endeavor was hardly a "first" in Hollywood filmmaking: it was an attempt to give the film the cachet other war films had achieved (D. W. Griffith's

*The Birth of a Nation* [1915] and Thomas Ince's *Civilization* [1916], for instance) by having the prestige of the author's name associated with it, just as Charlie Chaplin was associated, as a famous actor, with *Shoulder Arms* (1918).

The director King Vidor had made the great war epic *The Big Parade* in 1925. Starring John Gilbert and focusing on the adventures of an American unit in France, *Big Parade* was a boy-and-girl story, a wartime melodrama that, until *Front*, was the most popular success in that genre. As a silent film, however, *Big Parade* suffered from having come out during Hollywood's period of nostalgia toward the Great War, an interlude in which war genre films were made but war itself was highly romanticized and even sentimentalized. William Wellman's *Wings* (1927) was an air epic and thus almost unique in its class. To its credit, *Front* would avoid the clichés of previous war genre films, ranging from the lachrymose pacifistic theme of *Civilization*, in which Christ escorts a kaiser-double to the front, or those wartime scenes in *Big Parade* of dubious historical accuracy. As this brief survey of Hollywood war films can only indicate, both Universal's proposal and timing for its new film were opportune. The film and its subsequent production hold a unique place in American cultural history.

*Front* established the directorial career of Lewis Milestone, who was awarded the choice assignment over another director competing for the job, Herbert Brennon. A young unknown actor, Lew Ayres, played the role of Paul Baumer (the umlaut was dropped from the film name). Milestone had come to America in the early 1900s as a Ukrainian immigrant. He worked in the U.S. Signal Corps in 1917 and made contacts with the future film directors Victor Fleming and Josef von Sternberg. He earned the opportunity to direct Hollywood films after a rigorous apprenticeship in editing and screenplay writing. He once said that directing was "the easiest job in the world"; nevertheless, someone at Universal Studios was sufficiently impressed by the western front scenes in Milestone's wartime comedy *Two Arabian Knights* (1927) to offer him the film direction of *Front*.

The scripting, preparation, and filming of *Front* took about nine months. The total cost was $1,250,000, and the film was shot mainly in sequence at Universal Studios and on nearby Balboa Island. Battle scenes were done on the Irvine Ranch, about 50 miles from Hollywood. The script was a joint product of three talented artists, the writers Maxwell Anderson, George Abbot, and Del Andrews. As an experienced Hollywood journeyman and a hands-on director, Milestone's influence was never absent from the narrative and dialogue framework of the film. Milestone was especially concerned with the point of reference for a film with an implied pacifist theme. A way to establish the much needed realistic orientation of the story line finally emerged. The time frame would be chronological (not disjointed, as in the novel), not only to ease the understanding of the film audience but to provide a rationale for the changes within Paul. The film would start in school (another major change from the novel), then show the boys being recruited for the German army. Next would come boot camp training, followed by deployment to the front.

When Remarque's film was premiered in April 1930 at the Cathay Theater in Los Angeles, he had earned about $90,000 in royalties on the American book sales of *All Quiet*—a handsome amount for a previously unknown author. Plans were also made early in 1930 to issue a photoplay edition of the novel (including film stills) by the American publishing firm of Grosset & Dunlap. This less expensive edition was not sold through conventional bookstores and was intended to supplement the feature film's distribution in the United States (Firda 1988, 67). Photoplay editions of novel adaptations were then (as now) an effective segment of feature film merchandising of cinematic products. For Remarque, Universal Studios made a special effort to prime the American public for another *Big Parade* and even tried to compete with the newly released film version of R. C. Sheriff's English wartime play *Journey's End* (1928). *Front*'s pessimistic ending, however, set a new trend in American war genre films. It would be difficult to sell a film that debunked and demythologized the heroism of war. As the film critic Bosley Crowther notes, not only is there no triumphant conclusion or even Allied victory in *Front*, but the film asks an American movie audience to identify radically with a non-American hero, a German, and his comrades (79). Up to then, Hollywood had promoted the American belief that power, persistence, and military might were positive elements in national survival, and its films had always depicted a clear line of demarcation between the enemy and the side of justice. Milestone made the directorial decision to use a scenario that emphasizes the realism and tragedy of war in a way that transcends nationalist sentiments. Instead of a dying American soldier, the filmgoer sees only a soldier. The director hoped that the audience for the movie, like those who had bought the novel, would be motivated to hear its pacifist message transferred to the screen.

War in itself did not especially interest Milestone. What was important to him and to most of the viewers of the film was an individual soldier's response to war. Milestone agreed with Remarque's implied pacifism. In *Front*, Milestone functions as an *auteur*, a film director with an artistic and ideological program: to imply the horror of war. *Front* does not perpetuate the typical Hollywood exploitation of battle scenes and patriotic—however well-meaning—sentimentality. Remarkably, the film has no sustaining love interest, only ordinary soldiers, as John McCarten noted in a revival in August 1950, "to whom food [and the success of the general staff's battle plans are] more important than cosmic issues."[6] *Front* was awarded the Best Picture Oscar for 1929–30, an unusual accomplishment for a product of a patently commercial genre that more often featured romanticized combat, glory, and the excitement of military victory.

The continuity and subtitles consist of approximately 16 parts, which will be sketched below.[7] *Front*'s original running time was 140 minutes. Later releases in 1938 and 1950 were shortened, and an anti-Nazi prologue was added to the 1938 version. In the videotape version currently available, viewers can see all but four minutes of the original. Many of the characters in Remarque's book reappear in the film (variant spelling of some names): Paul Bäumer, Katczinsky, Gerard Duval, Tjaden, Müller, Albert, Leer, Behm, Kemmerich, Detering, Westhus, and Kantorek. Revealing its close thematic identification with the novel, the film begins with Remarque's disclaimer that "this story is neither an accusation nor a confession." Perhaps the most outstanding technical change Milestone made was shooting a scenario set within a chronological sequence of time. The progress of the story and the character development are logical and straightforward. No flashbacks interrupt the flow. Avoiding the novel's extended, often strained stream-of-consciousness style allows Milestone to offer the film viewer a developed middle narrative.

Part 1 opens in 1914 in a nameless German town; the citizens are waving at a crowd of passing soldiers. The butcher and the post-man, good citizens of the empire, are busy with their morning routine. Himmelstoss, the postman, is making plans to change his uniform the next day, that is, join the army. Kantorek, a conformist schoolmaster, is shown lecturing to his class, a captive audience, on the fatherland and the honor of the military. He slyly alludes to the talents of Paul Baumer, who has "great promise as a writer," but he intimates that Baumer's ambition is petty compared to the opportunity to sacrifice for one's country. Kantorek succeeds in his secret agenda of proclaim-ing that no more classes will be held while the war is being fought in France. Franz Kemmerich (one of the first to die on the western front) daydreams for a moment in a shot in which he looks down at his uni-form and sees the proud smile of his father. These shots are the filmic equivalents of the moments early in the novel when Bäumer remem-bers how he and his classmates were hectored and shamed into enlist-ing under a false kind of patriotism.

Parts 2 and 3 bring the boys forward in time to a basic training camp and their subsequent assignment to duty. They expect this pre-liminary training to be a game but find that their training sergeant, Himmelstoss, is a martinet who moves quickly to bring them under his control. He puts the boys in his battalion through their paces, through mud and slime. Himmelstoss vows to drain the mother's milk of kind-ness from their civilian lives. The resentment and bitterness of Himmelstoss's subordinates over his abuse of them is a theme in both the novel and the film. Milestone shows the insolence and the inequity of power under the German military system. The abused recruits catch Himmelstoss one night and drop him into muddy water. Their ordeal with him, however, is only a preliminary to the battlefield, their first assignment.

The boys are soon posted to an enemy town near the front that, as the viewer soon discovers, is an evacuation point for wounded sol-diers. There is a grim initiation scene: the dying soldiers are being unloaded from a troop train. Street scenes are intercut with close-ups of men and equipment. The surface activity belies the real danger of death, and shots are heard before the train pulls out. It is clear to the boys that they will be billeted close to the center of the conflict. At this point, Milestone introduces Katczinsky (Kat) to the film audience. Played by the veteran Hollywood actor Louis Wolheim, Kat is first seen, in a camera pan, hiding behind a wagon wheel and staring at a provision train where men are unloading dressed pigs. Kat reveals his "uncanny" ability to find food for himself and other hungry enlisted men when a man throws a pig to him. As in the book, Kat is the artful dodger, the seasoned veteran, and Paul Baumer's future friend.

Parts 4 through 6 contain three sequences that show the boys' first experience at the front. Kat becomes a leader and protector in the initial sequence, in which the boys are sent to lay barbed wire. Kat attempts to pass this assignment off as a routine trip into no-man's-land. Jokingly, he promises a clean change of underwear to any survivors of the night's activities. There is a medium shot of Paul turning about to view the departure of the truck that brought them to the front. Wire is unrolled, posts dug, and positions secured. Kat, sensing "trouble," is unable to forestall the first death. Behm, the last of the boys to join up, is the first to be killed. He is blinded and runs forward into the enemy's view, where he does a "dance" before dying. This death scene is not only an objective record of the facts of war, but a splendidly depicted moment of isolation in the conflict. Milestone, as Dorothy Jones has noted, unmasks the brutality of killing itself (275).

After the effect of Baumer's detail under fire has passed, the second sequence under battle fire opens. The boys are holed up in the trenches; they have spent five days under the sound of continual bombardment. Kat and his charges are sitting around playing cards, eating crusts of bread, and fighting off rats that, like the soldiers, are hungry and looking for food. When Paul complains of the "boredom," Kat notes that he told the boys this would be a "bad" war. In reality, however, Paul can barely disguise or hide his hysteria. This sequence features the breakdown of Franz Kemmerich in the dugout. Kemmerich tries to block the sound of falling bombs and fantasizes that Behm (now dead) wants his help. When Kemmerich makes two attempts to run out, he is shot in the leg by a French sniper. This illustrative scene in the film—absent in the novel—provides the rationale for Kemmerich's later confinement to a military hospital. The film audience is forced to enter a moral no-man's-land, and the boys are taught a hard lesson in personal survival and the absurdity of private heroics. As the film moves into the third battle sequence, Milestone's direction demonstrates that a soldier's life is anarchic and senseless, that his first and most important job is to protect himself against foolish exhibitionism as much as from the attack of the "enemy." The subsequent surface battle sequence is an impressively staged demonstration of the brute facts of hand-to-hand combat. Milestone's continuity records here a total of 177 scenes, alternating among close-ups in the trenches and shooting across the field and the front itself. A high open scene discloses that Paul's company is in the trenches and waiting for an advancing line of French soldiers. The director intercuts between both sides, and Paul takes his first shots at the French, who fall into the German wire entanglement. The viewer now understands why the wiring fatigue duty was so important.

Milestone shows the viewer that neither the French nor the Germans are final winners in the grim scenes of trench warfare. The French charge the German trenches but are beaten off and compelled to withdraw. The viewer, however, knows that regained frontal territory is only a temporary affair in the shifting theatrics of warfare. In fact, the film audience is comfortably neutral in its sympathies. The French and German military systems, not the individual enlisted men, are culpable in this visual display of waste and havoc. The first third of Milestone's film ends in an ethical and military stalemate. Paul and his group have been initiated into the elemental facts of war, and they have survived their early encounter with death and attendant hysteria.

Parts 7 and 8 feature the visit of Paul and his comrades to Kemmerich's bedside at a field hospital. This visit is an early highlight in the novel but is delayed in the film; in the latter medium, however, the sequence is expanded to include a cinematic "history" of Kemmerich's boots after he dies. Both the viewer and the reader remember that Kemmerich was very proud of the new pair of genuine leather boots given him by a relative. In the film, the boots are first mentioned at the start of military training, during which they symbolize

Kemmerich's good fortune in choosing to serve in the kaiser's army. In the hospital, however, Muller makes a claim for the boots after Kemmerich dies. Insensitively, Muller says to Kemmerich that he should leave them to "us" if he cannot "use" them. Dead men, of course, cannot wear boots. Why give the boots to an orderly? Muller's practical argument is hard to refute; in war, men and possessions are common barter. While Paul is getting the boots for his comrades, Kemmerich dies in his arms. To the viewer's horror, Paul discovers that the medics pay no attention to a dead soldier. Paul turns the boots over to Muller. Though the camera shows Paul only too glad to be alive—in contrast to Kemmerich—this is not the case with the later owners of Kemmerich's boots. Muller falls with a bullet in his shoulder. A boy named Peter wears the boots next, and he, too, is shot in the trenches while wearing them. These three men are shown as the doomed wearers of the boots in camera shots that are a montage of metaphors, signs of the war, fatally linked to the youth of the German empire. Stepping into another man's boots is a sentence of certain death, a foreshadowing of the war's collapse, and a totem of misfortune.

In the novel Remarque is careful to point out that, given the right context and the opportunity, the soldiers of warring nations can show tenderness and sympathy for one another. One such scene stands out in the film viewer's memory. It occurs in an especially ferocious episode in part 11 when Paul, in a lone encounter in a shell hole, stabs Gerard Duval, a French soldier, with his bayonet and then must spend the night with the dying Frenchman. There is no escape for Paul; overcome by pity despite himself, he begins to talk in a futile, compassionate way. The scene exposes both the propaganda and the mendacity of war. Milestone shows seven close-ups of the dying man, who alternates with Paul in the viewer's field of vision. Milestone also uses two-shots; as Andrew Sarris notes in an extended discussion on the effectiveness of this scene, if two figures are shown in the same frame, a visual bond is established between them.[8] Showing the developing bond of comradeship is precisely Milestone's thematic intention. As a 22-year-old actor, however, Lew Ayers could scarcely handle the sentimental, excessively literary language so fashionable in the 1930s (but barely acceptable later), as when Paul says: "Forgive me, comrade. Say that for me. . . . No, no. You're dead." A similar encounter between two enemy soldiers, one American and the other German, can be found in Vidor's *Big Parade*. While Milestone might be charged with "borrowing" from the earlier film, Paul's encounter with Duval is based directly on an episode in Remarque's book. Vidor's treatment comes off as more moving and cinematic, perhaps because *Big Parade*, a silent movie, is not handicapped by words, which Milestone, of course, had to use. Adding to the difficulty of the scene in *Front* is the great difference in ages between Ayers and the actor who played the dying Frenchman (Raymond Griffith). Sarris suggests rightly that Vidor's pair conveys more strongly the idea of vital youth wasted in war, while the Milestone pair seem to be abstract representatives of humanity rather than individuals.

Using parallel shots and sequences is one way in which Milestone emphasizes the redundancy of death and life in war. Echoing the earlier scene of Paul at the bedside of his dying friend Franz Kemmerich is the one of Paul himself getting wounded on a march to the front and being sent off to a hospital ward with his comrade Albert, who loses a leg. Paul manages once again to escape death and even amputation. The camera, in an exceptional instance of the cinematic legacy of the silent screen, captures here the wordless power of gestures and the profound sentiment in Paul's strained "Everything will be all right." That remark rings false to Albert, who glances down at a picture of himself and covers the lower half with his hand. Here the continuity calls for a fadeout, but we realize that Albert has learned the truth about his leg.

As does the novel, *Front* contains an extended sequence featuring Paul at home on leave. The opening shots show the streets of a sad, joyless town. A soldier is moving about on crutches, and civilians are simply moving about. Paul is seen walking along with bundles under his arm that, as the viewer learns later, are gifts of food for his sister and parents. The town is drained of the vitality and activity that marked the opening of the film. In a doorway the sight of a woman seated with her child seems to tell Paul what he does not need to know: people are hungry, poor, and suffering. His return home forces Paul to confront further the terrible truth about the spiritual and physical effects of the war not only on himself but on his school and his birthplace. This truth will separate Paul from his family (mother, father, and sister) and alienate him from his former existence as a schoolboy under Kantorek, his teacher. Paul becomes alienated from his mother's well-intentioned but overly simplistic words of affection and endearment. (Paul's mother was played originally by the actress Zasu Pitts, but her shots were rescheduled and the actress Beryl Mercer substituted.) Paul has seen and experienced too much of the authentic world of war, which has come to signify a permanent emotional division between himself and prewar Germany. His mother says to Paul that somehow she does not seem to know him. The war, the film makes clear, has alienated Paul from the comfortable and the familiar, with its bucolic patina. In the next scene Paul listens to his father's friends praise the "fortitude" and "loyalty" of the civilians. Those civilians make an argument for war and territorial conquest: Germany could make use of Belgium, the coal areas of France, and "some" of Russia. (In a splendid ironic turn of history, France would occupy parts of southwest Germany at the end of the war.)

Milestone added a sequence to Paul's leave not found in the novel. In a classroom visit to his old school, Paul finds his old teacher Kantorek, much to his disgust, lecturing the boys—at this late date in the war—about enlistment, for which the age is now 16 years. In contrast to the similar earlier sequence, the camera now shows Paul alone against the background of an empty street. But the teacher-chauvinist has the same captive audience: young boys on whose faces can be seen dreams of personal and national glory. The viewer is overcome by déjà vu. The truth is that it is dirty and painful to die for the fatherland. Paul's speech before his former teacher is an openly pacifist plea, a direct attack on the hypocrisy of a society that supports such a war. The novel and the film meet thematically at this point. As the critic Dorothy Jones observes, the camera emphasizes that the viewer has experienced the scene before, from the beginning of Kantorek's fraudulent appeal to heroism to its pitch of tragic, fateful repetition (278). Paul's refusal to support Kantorek is a dignified but futile gesture to undermine the war's cycle of killing. In that moment Paul realizes the joylessness and senselessness of his homecoming. He decides to return from leave four days early. The end of the leave sequence features a tender parting from his mother, but it is clear that Paul is eager to return to the front. As he may or may not know, this visit home will be his last.

Paul returns to the trenches and his comrades, but he finds his company decimated. Younger soldiers greet him as an old-timer, a survivor in a war that the Germans are losing. Paul finds his best friend, Kat, only to lose him when the sergeant is hit by flying shrapnel. Paul is bereft of not only a comrade but a brother. This scene is the second in the film in which Paul confronts death in a direct way that enlightens the viewer about the brotherhood of men. The deaths of Kat at the hospital dressing station and of the Frenchman Duval in a shell hole are parallel conditions under which men suffer and die. In both instances, Paul remains beside the dying man, an act of witness and compassion. Paul's last words to Kat, when he believes the older man is still alive, are pathetic and despairing: "You taught us how to dodge shells—my first bombardment. How I cried."

In the ending of *Front*, a structured buildup of camera shots leads the viewer toward Baumer's death on the front. We first see the empty wasteland of the war's frontier, then close-ups of Paul leaning against the wall of the trenches. A soldier in the foreground is scooping water with a shovel. Then the camera pans down to the ground, disclosing a butterfly that has settled on the lid of an old tin can. The viewer remembers an earlier shot, during Paul's visit home, of his schoolboy collection of mounted butterflies. It can only be Paul's hand reaching out for the butterfly, an expressive gesture toward a creature of beauty. This movement, however, puts Paul into the range of a French sniper. At the exact moment he touches the butterfly, he is shot down by the sniper. The famous final butterfly scene is, of course, not in the book but is instead a happy instance of visual inspiration. (It was purportedly suggested to Milestone by Karl Freund, the cameraman for F. W. Murnau's silent film classic *The Last Laugh* (1924). Remarque only notes in the novel that Bäumer falls forward. The montage of close-ups between Paul, intent on touching and preserving a timeless symbol of beauty and innocence, and the Frenchman, intent on killing, deconstructs wartime heroics and jingoism. Paul's death is signaled finally to the viewer by the shot of a drawn-back hand, a film image that bears wordless testimony to the silent screen.

Another film addition to the story's end is a scene superimposed on a battlefield of crosses. The faces of Paul, Kemmerich, and Muller turn back and join those of other marching German soldiers. Instead of a montage of announcements from the German War Office proclaiming that everything is "all quiet" on the western front, this strong visual superimposition of shots, in making the point that war is clearly a metaphor for death, allows no sentimental remission of the tragedy of war.

Such a pacifist film did not escape criticism in Germany. Universal Studios chose 4 December 1930 for the German premiere at the elegant Mozarthalle Theater on Nollendorfplatz in Berlin. German censors (in a city ruled by the liberal Socialist party) approved the release of the film in Germany, despite a protest by the Defense Ministry, whose representatives said that the film cast aspersions on the German army. Remarque's novel had already been subjected to the same charges of disloyalty and slander, so it was no surprise when, in a long article, the *New York Times* reported that the film "let loose a storm of controversy" seldom seen in a German city.[9] Even moderate German film critics were guided in their opinions by political rather than artistic considerations. Germans had seen only a toned-down, shortened version of *Front*, but nevertheless it was universally declared that an "enemy" had made another anti-German film. Right-wing Germans had still not forgotten their country's loss of national pride in World War I and the unprecedented humiliation of the German people. One German paper made a list of 21 American films that were clearly anti-German. There were calls in the Reichstag for the limitation of American film imports.

But the controversy over *Front* did not subside and became, in fact, an incident in the annals of the Nazi party, which would seize control of the German government only three years later. One day after the film's invitational premiere, Goebbels and 200 followers—in a sign of things to come—made a surprise appearance at the Mozarthalle Theater and, with the help of smelly bombs, white mice, and sneezing powder to throw around, ran amok through the audience. Only the Socialists, particularly the party's reigning intellectuals, some of whom were very left-wing, spoke up for the film and against the Weimar government's decision to stop showings for the immediate future. The centrist *Vossische Zeitung* reported that there was proof the National Socialists had planned the disruptive protest. The Nazis hoped to stop showings of *Front* entirely and to intimidate anyone trying to enter the theater. Goebbels's attitude toward the film's "shameful" portrait of German nationalism only complicated the German response to the film. He preferred to ignore the illegal nature of his assault on the right of freedom of assembly. In fact, Carl von Ossietzky, who died later in a Nazi concentration camp under the cruel punishment meted out to Hitler's enemies, accused the Weimar government of caving in to Goebbels, a "psychopath." The Weimar Republic, Ossietzky said, should have defended the film and acknowledged that both the book and the film were political events. The government's official censorship on aesthetic grounds was a very weak position for a democratic institution to take.[10]

The Berlin police chief, Albert Grzesinski, who was very much involved in the film scandal, noted in his memoirs that he would have permitted *Front* to be shown in Berlin indefinitely but the Weimar government made an unnecessary concession to the political right.[11] The Nazi protests in front of the theater gave the government an excuse to intervene for the sake of law and order. Goebbels, of course, had made his point and turned the government around, showing who was actually in control. The Socialist critic Walter Victor wrote perceptively in 1932 that other antiwar films had been shown without incident in German theaters, for example, William Wellman's *Wings* (1927) and G. W. Pabst's 1930 antiwar rebuttal to *Front*, the silent film *Westfront 1918*.[12] Like *Front*, *Westfront* deals with German soldiers engaged in trench warfare and failing to hold their own against French attacks. German and French soldiers die next to one another. In noting the seeming contradiction in the reception Germans gave to each of these antiwar films, Victor notes that the Ufa film studio, which produced *Westfront*, was owned by Alfred Hugenberg, a competitor of Ullstein Verlag, Remarque's publisher. Even though pacifist, *Westfront* had the imprimatur of its studio chief. What *Front* lacked,

Victor suggests, was the support of similarly powerful capitalist money that would back the release of any film it made

As a matter of historical interest, a French dubbed version of *Front* was shown for the first time in 1963 to a French audience. The initial premier showing in Paris on 1 December 1930 was of a silent version especially adapted in Hollywood. A scene in which German soldiers meet French girls was left out. The key scene in which Paul kills Gerard Duval was shortened. Film reviewers noted that the French audience looked on the film as peace propaganda and, to their credit, accepted its pacifist theme.

# 11

## Evaluation: *All Quiet on the Western Front* and Other German War Novels

Remarque was not the only German writer producing books about his experience as a combatant and observer in the First World War.[1] The books of other Germans were also famous and reviewed in newspapers and periodicals of the Weimar intellectual establishment. Some appeared before *All Quiet* was published in 1929, and, in fact, Remarque's book was measured against the steadily increasing number of war memoirs, reminiscences, and works of fiction that were finding favor with the German public. This chapter will briefly discuss three such texts that survive as landmarks in the history of the German World War I novel: Fritz von Unruh's *The Way of Sacrifice*, written in 1916, published in 1919; Ernst Jünger's *The Storm of Steel*, published in 1919 and a best-seller; and Ludwig Renn's *War*, which appeared in 1928, one year before *All Quiet*, and was the war book of preference among the German Weimar Left.[2] Remarque's book can then be placed within its unique literary and social context. All three of these books, like *All Quiet*, were based on autobiographical events, but each author presents quite a different narrative and analysis of his war experience. Each author, like Remarque, remains a distinguished figure in contemporary German literary history.

Remarque probably read each of these war novels. They represented sundry literary styles, ranging from fashionable expressionist melodrama (Unruh) to minimal realism (Renn). In addition, these books, like all German war texts, were ultimately influenced by the political prejudices of their authors. In Weimar Germany especially, commitment to a literary program like expressionism precluded allegiance to that program's sponsoring political doctrine that was often reformist and leftist oriented. Only Remarque managed to remain politically neutral in his famous book. Weimar-era German war novels were theoretically free of government censorship, and their authors (Ludwig Renn, for instance) claimed to be objective in recording both their personal and fictionalized wartime experiences. Literary history confirms, however, the inevitable political tendency in writing about a loaded subject like World War I, which had been an ineffable experience both for defenders of the Great War as a "primary" life force (Jünger) and for those who saw it as a communal descent into barbarism and mass delusion (Unruh). Those Germans who favored Remarque's book for its pacifism and solitary independence rejected Jünger's finely tuned and sensitive argument that the lost war had been a shining star on the horizon of the defeated German nation. Jünger's clever rhetoric defending war was a narcotic for mournful (and angry) Germans. The war, Jünger said, had been a storm signal and a prophecy of a new era. The experience of defeat had opened the eyes of German youth. A non-German reading Jünger, especially an American in 1920, would never have believed that the German empire had been humiliated and brought to its knees under the firm but eccentric terms demanded by the victorious Allies. In any event, Jünger's assessment of the recent conflict was fundamentally different from that of Unruh, who was one of the first of his generation to reject the jingoistic rhetoric of that war.

## FRITZ VON UNRUH, *THE WAY OF SACRIFICE*

Unruh, the son of a Prussian general, was born in 1885 (Pfeiler, 90). There was every expectation that the young man would follow a military career, and he enrolled at a training school at Plön in the state of Schleswig-Holstein (northern Germany). Like Ludwig Renn, whose family, social allegiances, and educational training were similar, Unruh resisted assimilation into the German ruling class. At Plön, Unruh's classmates were other nobility and the sons of the kaiser.

The young officer almost resigned his military commission in 1911, when his two plays *Officers* (1911) and *Prince Louis Ferdinand* (1913) were produced by the noted Austrian theatrical celebrity Max Reinhardt. *Officers* advocated an unconventional solution to the generational conflict between younger German officers and their older mentors. These two plays foreshadowed Unruh's disillusionment with the German officer class and its culpability in World War I. Unruh was informed that the military establishment disapproved of *Officers* and its implied message of passive resistance to army discipline, but he was sheltered from actual arrest. He received instead a writing assignment in February 1916 from a mentor who suggested that Unruh write a book for the German public about the German offensive against the French at Verdun.

Unruh took on the assignment and completed a work that exposed the absurd and appalling loss of life on the German side. Verdun was a great stalemate for the Germans in the Great War, for they never succeeded in breaking down the French defenses at a site sacred to French historical memory. Military losses and ephemeral victory characterized the changing fortunes of a battle that endured from February to June 1916. *The Way of Sacrifice* (1919) was probably the first major text written by a European about this crucial battle in the Great War. The last line of Unruh's book—which bears a simple dedication to his mother—testifies to its authenticity and the contemporaneity of the events he depicts: "In the field, before Verdun, Spring 1916" (WS, 181). The military court before which Unruh was ordered to appear totally rejected his unmistakably pacifist, utopian message. The short work of approximately 200 pages infuriated the German military, which had expected a propaganda piece. The "sacrifice" alluded to in the book's title is not an offering of a German hero's death for the kaiser and the German nation. It is rather a sacrifice for future humanity, a promise delivered by a "dead" German soldier to subsequent generations. Unruh depicted the battle at Verdun as an abstract struggle for moral enlightenment. War, he said, was a testing ground for men's ideals in a strife-ridden world. In the book a platoon leader rejects the militarist argument that fortresses or even nations loom high in the priorities of enlisted fighting men. As Pfeiler has noted, Unruh underwent a conversion: raised to believe in duty and honor according to the book, he struggled with that belief and finally rejected it, finding a spiritual meaning in the Verdun conflict in terms other than the stereotypical view of war as a bath of steel for the rebirth of the German people (91).

In contrast to *All Quiet*, *Sacrifice* does not have one central character. The book's point of view is projected onto a bevy of symbolic figures, each of whom has his turn as the author's voice before receding back into the anonymity of the conflict. The reader is urged to discern and discover war as a choral, communal experience. Captain Werner is a pessimistic but dutiful leader of men who nevertheless despises the hollow doctrine that a man will fight for the air he breathes, that in combat a man wants to prove what he is made of (WS, 63). The protean nature of Unruh's antiwar idealism is also exemplified in the platoon leader Clemens, who accepts death and dying as a price for human understanding and clarity, a preliminary step to a fraternity of the soul and spirit (WS, 67). A major difference between Werner and Clemens, however, is Clemens's refusal to accept war as a law of nature, or even Werner's notion about its inevitability. The reader soon discovers that Unruh explicates war as a dialectual philosophical struggle among ideas and ideologies, emerging from the carnage of war. Unruh's position is theoretical: he searches for a philosophical unity. In this very important way, Unruh was a dialectician of the war novel, while Remarque was not. Unruh allows, even encourages the expression of views both for and against war. His sergeant, Hillbrand, who supports the family hearth and the fatherland, abjures Clemens's doubts and pessimism and, in fact, perceives "the way of sacrifice" quite differently. For Clemens, Verdun will be a "threshing-floor of blood," while for Hillbrand, German men will fight anything that might destroy their faith in the primacy of ethnic survival.

## Evaluation: German War Novels

*Sacrifice* is divided into four parts: *Anmarsch* (Advance), *Schützengraben* (Trenches), *Sturm* (Storm), and *Opfergang* (Way of Sacrifice). The narrative trajectory of these four parts is slight but leads directly into the obvious end of the German attack on Verdun. "Advance" and "Trenches" contain loosely constructed scenes and episodes that reveal characters and their ideological worlds. When the book opens, it is January 1916 and a group of soldiers is being driven to an unknown destination (*WS*, 3). Verdun and major and minor characters are introduced to the reader. Clemens has a dream about the twisted and convoluted roads leading to Verdun. In the dream the roads are distant avenues ominously perceived as mangled snakes. The dream is a striking and memorable premonition of future struggle and possible defeat. The first part of Unruh's book ends, ironically, with Clemens receiving orders to act as a company guide over the roads and villages of the French countryside. He finds it impossible to overcome his feeling of foreboding over the outcome of the Verdun battle.

"Trenches" moves into an account of army routine that authors of German war novels never failed to include (*WS*, 59). The reading public absorbed the details of the *Stellungskrieg* (trench or positional warfare) in which foot soldiers dug their own trenches; an elaborate system of trenches emulated the infrastructure of a modern city. Jünger's *Steel* and Renn's *War* also feature extensive commentary on trench life. Remarque elaborates, too, on the continual boredom and subsequent "madness" of this particular kind of forced communal living. In the trenches in World War I German soldiers learned to suppress both ego and individuality. "Trenches" lays out the central philosophical and ethical issues of war.

Unruh handles characterization through devices such as extended monologues, which the reader finds throughout "Trenches." Werner, however, never verbalizes his thoughts before his subordinates. An inner monologue reveals him to be a contemplative man who feels that the loss of young German soldiers is not worth the "gift" of a victory in the Verdun battle. As an introvert, he would prefer to remain detached from army logistics. He is characterized

by Unruh as "sharing" the suffering of war but *never* the comradeship of men fighting for reasons of simple patriotism. He remains
deeply pessimistic and grieves over the outcome of the fighting at
Verdun.

The setting for "Storm" and "Way of Sacrifice," the last two
parts, is the battle itself. The initial stages of the German attack on
Verdun are clearly differentiated from the later phase, when the
German side suffered great losses. As Werner gives his men the signal
to attack, Hillbrand jumps out of his trench with an ax in his hand.
Clemens moves forward like a crouching panther, throwing bombs
into the enemy line. The cadet Preis dashes about carrying out the captain's orders. Slaughter and havoc are the rule of the day. The
"wounded forest," the setting for the battle, lies comatose, a "shriek-
ing giant" (*WS*, 129). Unruh personifies and transforms the conflict
into a dying colossus. Hillbrand is the first to die, felled to the ground
like a tree. Realistic description blends with visionary ecstasy. Werner
is shot during an enemy gas attack, and by the end of the book only
Clemens, whom Unruh calls "the man of the spirit," is left to move the
platoon a mere three yards forward.

*Sacrifice* emphasizes the tragedy of Verdun as a German defeat,
as an event of historical magnitude. Like Remarque, Unruh is not concerned with conventional concepts of individual heroism. There are
only antiheroes in the final encounter at Verdun. But Unruh also does
not focus on one man's evolution, as Remarque does. From the beginning, Unruh shows the reader that his book lacks a protagonist. He
infers "we" more often than "I," and he identifies with the war experience of the group. In *Sacrifice* individual experience is seen in the context of shared transcendent values; physical and spiritual individuality
are secondary. How can a contemporary reader approach this war
novel whose theme is assimilating a realistic depiction of war into a
utopian scheme of social regeneration?

The German critic Ludwig Harig, in a recent assessment of
*Sacrifice*, notes correctly that its continuing appeal as an antiwar text
lies in its philosophical and linguistic bond with German literary
expressionism.[3] Unruh's ideology and language are derived from the

literary and political program of that early twentieth-century German creative movement. German expressionist writers were especially concerned with moral principles, that is, with renewing man himself. As the author of an antiwar novel, Unruh used expressionist principles to speak to his contemporaries, the German public, and other sympathetic listeners, but his call for spiritual regeneration was actually directed toward the widest range of humanity (*die Menschheit*). Zealously reformist, Unruh literally and ideally called for the birth of a new humanity out of the conflict of war, even in an "unavoidable" tragedy like Verdun.

Unruh and Remarque would have agreed on the hollowness of conventional notions of German wartime heroism and heroic deaths. Unruh, writing his little book at least ten years earlier than Remarque, placed his hope in a newly spiritualized German and international society, one emerging like the proverbial phoenix from the debacle of the Great War's battles. In the wider context of German literary history, Unruh reiterated the urgent vision of central expressionists (the Austrian poet Georg Trakl, the German poet Georg Heym, the German dramatist Reinhard Sorge) and located the dark powers of modern German industrial life in the battlefields of war. That vision led him naturally and inevitably into an expressionist analysis of the Great War. The events of *Sacrifice* stress conflict, contradiction, paradox, and crisis, all of which are also deliberately, and expressionistically, embodied in Unruh's characters.

Only then does Unruh find and examine the dynamism necessary for German inner and social rebirth. In this quest, his ecstatic, expressionist, and telegrammed language plays no small role. Nouns (names) and verbs (activity) in the novel compete for dominance as concepts of stability and change. The author's realistic account of the life-and-death struggle of Verdun is balanced stylistically by the expressionist pathos of his utopian worldview. Expressionist words and the ideals they incorporate mean more than the material remnants of the Verdun defeat. In the author's futuristic resolution of martial conflict, the facts and details of military maneuvers and bureaucratic rulings will fail the test of time.

# Ernst Jünger, *The Storm of Steel*

Ernst Jünger, the author of *The Storm of Steel* (1920), was born in 1895 in the city of Heidelberg. His father was a pharmacist, and his mother doted on him. The family was financially comfortable, though not excessively so, and lived according to prescribed social conventions. Jünger's family background was thus very different from that of Remarque, who could not expect any material or financial assistance from his impoverished parents. Jünger was deeply attached to a younger brother, Friedrich Georg, whose career as a well-known poet began after an army tour in the Great War. (Jünger mentions his brother in an episode of *Steel*, when Ernest takes extraordinary measures to save his brother's life [*SS*, 170].) In 1913 Jünger ran away from home to join the French Foreign Legion. He was 18 years old, and joining the legion was an exemplary instance of youthful rebellion against German schooling and family pressures, as well as the crystallization of his dreams of travel and French African adventures. His father's influence with the authorities rescued him from a signed contract. Jünger's African fling stamped his character and influenced his future writing: in *Steel* and other texts, hazard, venture, risk, and daring function as thematic devices. Jünger became the quintessential German defender of war and combat as a physical adventure and a spiritual odyssey. As a 30-year old writer and honored German officer, Jünger remembered his early African folly as a symbolic flight for freedom and act of rebellion against the fustian quality of Prussian life. He found a link between French Foreign Legion service in Oran and on the island of Chateau d'If and German army duty on the western front. For Jünger, military duty was a rite of passage.

When the First World War ended, Jünger had served almost four years of active duty. As a shock troop officer, he was hardened by his wartime experience. Jünger's combat encounters were more extensive than Remarque's. He deliberately sought out confrontations in battle with the enemy and was wounded many times, after which he endured periods of hospital recuperation. He was given the *Pour le mérite*, the highest Prussian award for personal bravery. Like Remarque, Jünger went to serve his country as a schoolboy but only after graduation from a secondary school. His war experience, however, formed him differently; unlike *All Quiet*, *Steel* will stand forever as a model text of the German frontline soldier. An essential narrative difference between *All Quiet* and *Steel* is that the latter was written from the viewpoint of a German combat officer, not that of an enlisted man. Remarque's book is the record of a common soldier's disintegration on the battlefield of an "anonymous" war. Jünger sees the war from a different perspective, a nationalist and militarist one.

At first, however, Jünger's defense of war and soldiering found no ready publisher in the Weimar press establishment. He was forced to resort to self-publication. A privately printed 1920 edition had to search for its own readership, which did materialize after the book became an underground success. In some quarters, *Steel* ran up against the antiwar mood of the liberal German Left. Unruh's expressionist appeal for the rebirth of humanity through an end to war and Remarque's pacifist work were more appealing to the left-leaning public emerging from the ruins of war. Liberals were skeptical of Jünger's argument that in the eyes of history, the defeat of the German army would be declared a victory. In the preface to *All Quiet* Remarque had claimed the opposite, namely, that the war had been a useless adventure, a fraudulent illusion for the "lost generation" of survivors. Jünger's appeal to the judgment of history, however, came at a time when many leaders of the Weimar government were casting their lot with the liberal protest in the literary and political arenas. Lines were drawn between Jünger's seemingly nonapologetic stance on German militarism and the defeated German army, on the one hand, and the equally rigid stance of the antiwar movement, on the other. By the 1930s a quarter of a million copies of *Steel* had been printed. German nationalists and the nascent Hitler movement tried to claim Jünger as a founding father of the totalitarian Right.

*Steel* was based on an autobiographical source: a personal diary that Jünger also used for later essays he wrote on the nature and protocol of war.[4] His first book, however, straddled the line between documentary and fiction. In subsequent editions of *Steel* Jünger excised many references to himself in the text, especially those that seemed immodest. Later readers would also find a more focused narrative strategy, along with greater stylistic directness and simplicity. Jünger expounded on the psychology and spiritual life of his ideal German soldier in his 1930 essay "Der Krieg als inneres Erlebnis" (War as an Inner Experience).[5] "Experience" is, in fact, a complementary text to the purportedly realistic account in *Steel* of the author's service on the western front as a combatant functioning within the structure of daily military routine and army discipline. Despite Jünger's undiluted patriotism, his conclusions about Germany's role in the Great War are ambiguous, as the English critic R. H. Mottram observed in a preface to the first English translation of *Steel*. Mottram recommended the book to English-language readers only reluctantly; he lamented its factual mistakes, along with its puzzling inclusion of aesthetic observations on the landscape of the western front (*SS*, vi). According to Mottram, Jünger seemed to think that Nietzschean heroics could be reconstructed from gas masks and army shrapnel. Mottram remarked further that Jünger's literary images reflect combat fever, mental derangement, and "overworked" fantasy. The cultural and literary gulf between English and German writing about the Great War was thus clearly apparent, even after a decade of peace between the two nations. Jünger could only reply that the war had been a "marvelous schooling" of the heart and that confronting the enemy contributed to the moral evolution of the German soldier (*SS*, xii).

*Steel* is divided into two parts: the accounts of trench fighting, (*Grabenkämpfe*), and the discussion of the war weaponry that forced changes in combat logistics (*Materialschlacht*). Jünger's many chapters on these themes cover important historical battles on the western front: Guillemont (August 1916), the Somme (1916), and Langemarck (Flanders). The decisive March 1918 offensive fought at St. Quentin between the Germans and the English, described by Jünger as a "gigantic roar of annihilation," is the subject of an extended chapter (*SS*, 250). For Jünger, the chief purpose in recounting these battles is to use them as settings in which soldiers' martial feelings and other emotions are truly tested. Hand-to-hand combat under the duress of warfare frees the flow of blood in a German soldier from the "bondage" of the restrictive life in the trenches, the sterile routine of which has already been introduced in the early chapters "Orainville," "Les Eparges," and "Douchy."

As Mottram observed, Jünger adopts a unique writerly strategy in the initial stages of his text; an incident in "Les Eparges," for instance, is important in that it shows the particular aesthetic drift of Jünger's book. Jünger reports that one morning he jumped out of his trench and into the morning mist (*SS*, 21). He found himself standing in front of the greenish-white corpse of a dead Frenchman. The enemy soldier was surrounded by other rotting bodies, all of which formed a "field" of great proportions. Jünger, however, was attracted to the beauty of the scene and decided to linger. A shudder of aesthetic recognition runs through his thoughts and emotions. He confesses (to the reader and himself) that the promised carnage of war was part of what attracted his generation to the military experience. In the manner of a confessional reverie, Jünger notes that the conformist, bland tone of life in Wilhelmine Germany had induced a hunger in German youth for the "perversity" of war (*SS*, 23). In the rest of this trench episode Jünger strives to find a mental and emotional haven within himself for the dislocated body parts, the ugly colors of human decay in war. He takes a perilous stroll by the trench, oblivious to enemy guns and fire, stealing the booty of the defunct corpses. He rationalizes his conduct as true to the code of the victor reaping the spoils of war. The rotting trenches are an undeniable loss for the French side, but the Germans, especially Jünger, are "rewarded" by the images and patterns they present of life at the borderline of extinction. Jünger walks away with a pocketful of French cartridges and a fine striped shirt. He reads a few French newspapers and lights his pipe. For a moment, the war is suspended in chronological time and the author lectures the reader on the art of war. The reader finds out only later that Les Eparges was Jünger's first battle. His supple literary style in this passage is deceptively straightforward, his connoisseur's eye for selective detail serving to cleverly distract the reader.

Ever the creative aesthetician of the war experience, Jünger is so sensitive to the romance of war that he almost loses touch with the reality of the hostilities. This is stunningly evident in a key chapter, "Douchy and Moncy," in which the reader is diverted by Jünger's narrative description of the "ruins" of these two German-occupied French villages (*SS*, 31–45). His tone, both sentimental and picturesque, expresses the longing of a modern-day romantic for a lost historical time. Douchy and Moncy are in fact the headquarters and sites of German reserve fighting units. Both villages lie in the undulating country of Artois, an area of retreat and recuperation for German soldiers. Jünger notes the sight of a lonely light at the entrance to nighttime Douchy, which represents home and hearth to the fighting soldier, a place to sleep free of anxious dreams. Douchy has a reading room, a café, and a "vicarage garden." German officers and men drill in the "games" of war and drink in traditional German style. Jünger seems to welcome the decline of Douchy into a subliminal state, a condition that follows as the French inhabitants revert to a primitive (aesthetic) existence on the fringes of the former village. He marvels at how Douchy returns to its past and, in his eyes, becomes a model for a Socialist community. He and his comrades buy and barter eggs and butter from the natives. Among the very real signs of fighting and destruction, Jünger notes the compelling pattern of torn rifle packs and broken weapons among the onions, wormwood, and daffodils. He wonders how he can avoid meditating on the unexpected "beauty" of war, the inevitable effects of historical necessity and devastation.

In discussing *Materialschlacht*, Jünger records certain historical changes that signaled the beginning of modern mechanized warfare. Both Remarque and Jünger mention in their respective texts the initial trauma of gas warfare. In the latter stages of the Great War massive attacks on the enemy were often forced by the overwhelming use of heavy weaponry. Historians of war strategy have noted that the introduction of such weaponry diminished the role of the individual combat soldier. The die was cast, and the new goal of total destruction prevailed over the earlier ideal of seeking victory through personal combat. Cavalry fighting units gave way to greater and faster transport modes. Weaponry fire and troop movement became the basic elements of modern fighting strength that spelled victory over the enemy. If movement was halted and an advance prevented, weapons and firing could then increase from massed infantry and artillery units. The new logistics of such combat tactics are duly noted in Jünger's book.

# Evaluation: German War Novels

Jünger's discussion of the new weaponry reflects his assumption that the changes altered the rules of warfare forever. The swift and violent tempo of mass destruction, Jünger notes extensively in the "Overture to the Somme Offensive" and "Guillemont" chapters, brought on the death of the chivalrous ideal. In future wars, he asserts, it will be impossible to behave according to standards of gallantry and generosity toward one's enemy; the antagonist will be the massed fighting unit (*SS*, 110). To his credit, Jünger addresses the issue of British military heroism, the inspirational stand of British fighting units. But noble and altruistic feeling will end when others are confronted with new weaponry and the pointed German steel helmet. Jünger believed that the permanent change in the rules and adventure of war was personified both in the change in the outward physical appearance of the European fighting soldier and with the development of deadlier combat.

In the last chapter, "My Last Storm," Jünger attempts to justify the tremendous numbers of German soldiers lost during the 1916 Battle of the Somme, as well as at Guillemont and St. Quentin. He argues that the recent heroic war adventure was executed by the nation for pure and bright national aspirations and that the forfeiture of a million lives was a small price to pay for renewed German identity and national pride. But Jünger also pleads for the viability of higher values and principles that, in the end, are more significantly embodied in each individual than in the temporal life of the nation. Here the subtlety and complexity of Jünger's argument for war (and combat) bear close attention: the Great War was, he says, not only a grand opportunity for men to rise and fall as victors and losers for a patriotic cause, but more importantly, a unique, personal path to emotional and spiritual development. German soldiers lived in the mud of the trenches and witnessed the deaths of their comrades, but their faces and final thoughts were turned to the heavens (*SS*, 316). Jünger's ecstatic language compares the defeated German soldier to others who have harbored secret strength—a stoic Roman fighter or a martyred Christian. For Jünger, war is both a metaphor and the origin of one's reality, a primal source that also bears the seed of inevitable destruction. This destruction, in turn, is the first step in a renewal process.

As a classic explicator of war and fighting and the author of an important text on the Great War, Jünger gives that war a metaphysical and aesthetic foundation that is lacking in the commentary of liberal and Socialist critics, even that of Unruh and Remarque. The grand coda of the last chapter of Jünger's book anticipates, even welcomes, another European war. Though Jünger tried to purge some of the rhetoric of *Steel*'s closing passage in later editions, he never abjured the passionate ideas behind it. It is up to each reader to decide whether *Steel* pleads a particular political or philosophical agenda. Jünger sensed quite correctly that most surviving German soldiers sought "justification" for what they had endured. *Steel* is such a book and thus appealed to a conforming frontline soldier.

Jünger, however, was wrongfully claimed by the Nazis as a progenitor of totalitarian thought. His *Auf den Marmorklippen* (On the Marble Cliffs, 1939) was both humanistic and antithetical to Nazi doctrines of totalitarian rule and submission. For many reasons, Jünger's place in the history of modern German literature, especially the war novel, remains controversial. But he was clearly an original figure who can rightfully be placed at the opposite end of the spectrum from the pacifist Remarque.

# LUDWIG RENN, *WAR*

Remarque's *All Quiet* examines the roots of alienation in the lost generation of young German combatants, while Jünger's book became the classic text for a right-wing faction of defenders of war. Jünger described the war experience as tied to laws of nature and as therefore an ideal arena for growth and regeneration. A number of other German war novels looked at war in an entirely different way. These novels claimed to give impartial, objective accounts of the war on the western front. Devoid of any philosophical or political profundities, they were distinguished mainly by their portraits of war as an overwhelming reality and by their protagonists' direct and immediate submission to it. The authors of these novels were realists of a special persuasion. They took the point of view of an eyewitness to a crime or an accident. Their readers encountered an unstudied acceptance of war and very little introspection or sentiment. Such acceptance differs markedly from Jünger's reasoned analysis of war as a primal and therefore indispensable experience, or even Remarque's tragic sense of war as loss and deprivation.

An outstanding example of this third kind of war novel is Ludwig Renn's *War* (1929). "Ludwig Renn" was actually a pseudonym for Arnold Vieth von Golssenau, who was born in Dresden in 1889.[6] *War*, like Remarque's best-seller, became famous beyond Germany's borders. It presented the German enlisted man's leading role in the Great War from a unique point of view. Renn never points an accusing finger at the principal culprits in the war, the German upper class, as Remarque does often in *All Quiet*, and his plain-speaking protagonist—also named Ludwig Renn—was spared charges of treason by the German Right. *War* is written in the style and format of a chronicle. Even some of the most annihilating battles of the Great War (the Somme, Aisne-Champagne) are rendered without sentiment or didacticism. The facts and details of Renn's broad presentation are meant to speak for themselves. *War*, however, was read by the German Left as an antiwar text, and the noted leftist novelist and critic Arnold Zweig (*The Case of Sergeant Grischa*, 1928) praised *War* over *All Quiet* because of what he interpreted as Remarque's decision to avoid the political fallout from his book (597). Renn did not protest a political reading of his book, while Remarque clearly disavowed politics. Zweig noted that only a war sympathizer would fail to note the superior antiwar tenor of Renn's book.

Renn was born in the protected and privileged setting of German Saxon nobility, an existence far removed from that of his fictional hero in *War*, the carpenter Ludwig. Renn's titled father was a skilled instructor of military history to the children of Saxon rulers. His mother traced her Eastern European heritage to a long line of German merchants in Moscow. Renn's autobiographical books *Adel im Untergang* (The Demise of the Nobility, 1944) and *Meine Kindheit und Jugend* (My Childhood and Youth, 1957) discuss the conflict between his mother's cultural identification with Slavic Russia and the social aspirations of his Saxon German father. His father had abandoned an officer's career for teaching, and craving the high cachet of military fame and honor, he expected his son Arnold to fill the painful void left in his life.

But there was another source of strife in the young author's life: the alienating and authoritarian regimen of the German school system. This system, as Renn noted elsewhere, perverted the ideals of classical humanism as it redirected them into martial service to the government.[7] The chauvinistic and paramilitary teaching of the German gymnasium was a prelude to the disciplined and structured character of Prussian and Saxon life. Renn saw himself as an early rebel against German education. In the opening pages of *All Quiet* Paul Bäumer also complains about the alienating system of German pedagogy, which failed as a guide and mediator through the initial stages of the Great War. Though his novelistic character does not recover from that failure, Remarque himself never ceased to criticize the deficiencies of German society and culture. For Renn, on the other hand, the Great War held different revelations. It opened his eyes to the world of proletarian life, the egalitarian existence of "invisible" common men, as he had never seen it before. This slow and deliberate learning experience led Renn away from his special officer's status in the Saxon Guards into becoming an active fighting soldier on the western front. He was one of the very few German officers in the Great War who shared the dangers of open combat with his subordinates and, in doing so, underwent a profound psychological and emotional metamorphosis. His allegiance to his upper-class heritage disappeared and his regard for the working class deepened ("Nachwort," 520). Renn was drawn to the straightforward warmth and love of the "nameless" German soldier on the western front, living in dirt, rain, and danger. His experiences in the Great War would alter his life forever and eventually inspire him to join the Weimar working class.

Renn cast the fictional hero of *War* as a soldier from the masses, an artless carpenter whose individuality lies in his virtual anonymity. If the looming presence of Jünger's officer never disappears from the pages of his text, the reader of *All Quiet* is likewise convinced that the novel rises or falls on the success of Remarque's sensitive characterization of Paul Bäumer. Renn, however, was attracted neither to Jünger's sentimental aestheticism nor to the existential dread of life Bäumer experiences in the final days of the war. *War* emphasizes realistic detail and the sober truth about fighting on the front. The protagonist Ludwig never refers to the future superfluous status of his generation. Renn's rigid and sanitized presentation of his hero reflected his rejection of any political or social platform, though his readers were "free" to draw their dissimilar conclusions. This apolitical tendency, however, would change in the future. In 1930 Renn published a sequel to *War* called *Nachkrieg* (After the War), in which he relates Ludwig's return home from the hostilities. *After the War* autobiographically records Renn's later evolution as a Communist sympathizer and party loyalist. In the Nazi period Renn was forced into exile in Mexico. With the founding of East Germany, Renn entered the German Socialist pantheon of that country's literary canon.

In 1916 Renn began to write down his wartime impressions, but probably because of his sensitivity about being an amateur writer, these were never intended for publication. He did not complete a final manuscript of *War* until 1924, several years after his return from the war. The work is divided into three parts: "Vormarsch" (Advance), "Stellungskreig" (Trench War), and "Zusammenbruch" (Collapse). The shortest part is the last one. "Trench War" contains subsections on life in the trenches at Chailly, the Battle of the Somme (obligatory in most German war books), the Aisne-Champagne battle in 1917, the trench war of 1917–18, and the March offensive in 1918. Renn's parts and subsections correspond to the important subject units in Jünger's *Steel*. By contrast, Remarque left out references to particular battles, a telling omission in the eyes of those critics who pointed out his lack of actual combat experience and the limited scope of Paul Bäumer's point of view.

Renn's book, using a first-person narrator, never strays from its introductory tone of brevity and simplicity. There one reads: "When the day of mobilisation came I was a lance-corporal" (*W*, 9). Ludwig is thus "set" in his novice role as a reporter and eyewitness to what follows. No time is "wasted" on a farewell ceremony between Ludwig and his mother. The lance-corporal and his comrades anticipate being assigned to duty on the eastern front, but instead they are driven by troop train to the banks of the Rhine, from where they begin their long march toward the Belgian frontier. They ascend heights and descend into villages. The German soldiers with their unshaved faces stare at the unfriendly Belgians. Renn does not explain the politics behind Germany's initial strategy of invading Belgium. Belgium, in fact, was only a transitional country from which the German military plan was to launch a lightning attack on France. Anticipating France's defeat, Germany was gambling on a quick victory in this first phase of the war.

As a foot soldier, Ludwig finds himself assigned to patrol near the Belgian River Maas (Meuse), the site, as it turns out, of his first battle (W, 24). He encounters fear and cowardice on both sides. In a carefully stated challenge to a tenet of the normally inflexible German military law—namely, that captured enemy prisoners must be shot—Ludwig suggests an alternative scheme and saves the lives of a group of Belgian civilians. He is soon overwhelmed by contradictory feelings over the dearth of heroic deeds during these early days of fighting. He dreams of escape from Belgium and welcomes the sight of the French frontier (W, 52). His reaction, however, shows the reader that he remains in the grip of war morbidity and psychological depression. He feels that southern German soldiers are superior to those of other German regions because they live the war in "cheerful ways" and respond to death and dying as the normal consequence of doing the day's business. Ludwig also learns a moral wartime lesson from his platoon officer, namely, that only "free" German soldiers, not "half prisoners" of the German military code, can be led into battle against the enemy. This officer is willing to overlook an instance of an enlisted man's deliberate refusal to follow orders (W, 84). For a brief moment, the young lance-corporal Ludwig lives out his original dream of achieving universal and national peace through war and higher necessity. This is an illusion, however, of which he will be disabused.

The "Trench War" part of Renn's novel gives the reader a detailed and objective accounting of several key battles of the Great War on the western front (W, 131). This part, the heart of the book, stresses the importance to the changing nature of the conflict of the battles of the Somme, the Aisne-Champagne, and the 1918 offensives.

Renn moves forward chronologically in these vital chapters. The reader sees what Ludwig sees with his cameralike eye. The lengthiest inventories of battle events are those devoted to the Somme and Aisne-Champagne. The initial section, "The Trenches before Chailly," allows Renn's narrator to pause and reflect (however briefly) on the process of inner change within himself, on his developing storm of self-doubt and examination. *War*, no less than *Sacrifice* and *Steel*, turns on the notion of wartime duty and experience on the front contributing to the process of self-education and change. The war, say these novels, changed every combatant and survivor. At one point in *War* Ludwig notes his turn away from false heroics after his company's unchallenged crossing of the River Maas in Belgium. The inanity of trench warfare has supplanted the false hopes of early German victories. But this highlighted moment of confessional doubt does not mean that the war is over yet for Ludwig.

Ludwig is assigned clerical duties for a time in the battalion library, and here Renn makes an indirect reference to his own daily chronicling of his war experience (*W*, 160). The reader, however, never learns exactly why Ludwig (Renn) *begins* to write. Is he driven, one wonders, by a historical sense of time or a passion for an accurate record? Renn reveals to his reader only infrequently the literary method behind *War*. What seems to be only a documentary accounting of Ludwig's wartime experience of the conflict on the western front is in fact, as the "Trenches before Chailly" section reveals, an unparalleled opportunity to gain insight into Renn's realist aesthetics, to understand finally how he differs from Remarque, Unruh, and Jünger. In "The Trenches before Chailly" the reader learns, for example, that Ludwig has tried for the "third" time to write down his account of the German battle at Lugny in 1914 (*W*, 160). The reader can thus conclude that the original purpose of *War* to be no more than an objective account underwent text revision (no less than other wartime German novels). At home on leave, Ludwig gives in to his mother's request to keep everything he has written up to the first battle of the Marne.

Renn, through his spokesman-narrator Ludwig, follows two fundamental rules of writing: there must be a nonarbitrary order to the words of a sentence, and this order is based on the reader's emotional response to those words. First the writer imagines the whole scene. He next notes the light and the shade, the sound and the emotional reaction. Only when all preliminary aesthetic and sensual phases of the planned text are exhausted can that writing begin (W, 160). These brief passages (*War*, 160) show that Renn, having deliberately left out everything not necessary, expected a certain readership for his book. An astute reader, however, will perceive the analogy between Ludwig's admitted failure to find the "right" words for his far-ranging thoughts and Renn's personal struggle to make sense of those German social and political changes that made World War I a watershed of history. Renn wrote his book not only to document the facts of wartime combat but also to record his personal and philosophical evolution. During a trip home Ludwig opens a family album and stares for a long time at a picture of his father as a young man. For the first time he feels a filial and emotional bond between his father and himself. The moment of bonding for both men may have been when each discovered he could go no further in answering life's momentous questions.

On 26 September 1916 Ludwig receives his orders for the Battle of the Somme. Begun in July 1916 by the Allies to relieve pressure on the French army at Verdun, the battle was one in which the Germans gave little ground to enemy forces. Ludwig's battalion holds itself in readiness 12 miles behind the fighting. Though history records that the German army had a great victory at the Somme, Renn's book presents the conflict from a less glorious point of view (W, 165). A preponderance of dialogue reveals the human dimensions of the battle. Smoking and drinking disguise the anguish and hysteria at the prospect of being taken prisoner. Ludwig's hair stands on end when he hears stories of "fabulous" German heroics. He is aghast when a lieutenant-colonel corrects his foolhardy battle readiness, and he dreams of his own crucifixion. He overhears defeatist conversation by men of the second company. French reconnaissance planes fly "insolently" above the German trenches; no German aircraft can be seen. Ludwig curses the swagger of the German airman. The French begin to throw gas bombs, and all signs indicate another long battle, as at Verdun. Ludwig is wounded and taken to a hospital where, in a fit of delirium, he refers to the "absolutely splendid" stand of the German army. His doctors, however, challenging his extravagant choice of words in recounting the number of German dead, ascribe his state to a kind of overwrought ecstasy (W, 202). They are not deceived by the truly tragic dimensions of this decisive battle. Renn allows their antiwar criticism to rest as a matter of record. As an author, however, Renn differs from Remarque in the manner and tone with which he handles this wartime episode ("Wounded"). The recovering Ludwig, for example, unlike Paul Bäumer in the hospital, receives human warmth and consideration from the doctors and staff. He is even befriended by an army captain, though Ludwig is "puzzled" by this unexpected gesture of good feeling from an officer; it crosses the lines of protocol. When he has recovered, Ludwig is promoted to corporal and then sent off to the expected French spring offensive on the Aisne River.

The conclusion of *War* reveals signs of a breakup in the ranks of the surviving 1917 German army. Ludwig hears that German Alsatians have deserted to the winning French (Allied) side. Renn also refers to the growing enmity in the last years of the war between the frontline fighters and the officer staff. The book shows how the introduction of trench warfare accelerated a growing division between fighting and logistical units. The men who put their lives on the line complain about the safe positions of the military theoreticians. The German officer gradually loses his exalted status in Ludwig's eyes. One such figure is Lieutenant Lössberg, a corrupt and ambitious man, a writer of long reports. Ludwig is also angry at the army chaplain who suggests to the men that Germany hold on to Belgium after the war (W, 305). In October 1918 German enlisted men begin to talk of deserting, and Ludwig is wounded once more and receives the Iron Cross of the First Class. This award concludes his active service. He is one of the last of the German troops moving forward in front of advancing French and Belgians.

Renn's narrator undergoes growth and inner change in the context of a picaresque tale of adventure and peril. Ludwig's perception of the war and wartime experience is at first conditioned by his mind, which, like a tabula rasa, is an open field for sensations and feelings. He seems ready to learn from his role as a combatant and enlisted soldier. The reader then realizes that Ludwig protects himself, with increasing facility, against the intrusion of the negative side of war out of his innate ability to make the best of a bad situation. Renn alludes to the possibly picaresque nature of Ludwig's role in a telling scene ("The Aisne-Champagne Battle") in which an officer friend gives him a copy of the 1668 German novel *Simplicius Simplicissimus*, a classic book that offers a realistic account of an innocent survivor (a figure like Ludwig) of Germany's tragic Thirty Years' War (W, 252). Ludwig tries to read the book but does not finish it. He fails to grasp the intended connection between the protagonist of that novel and himself. His friend had said only that the book would "suit" him. Like Simplicius, however, Ludwig dodges combat blows, is not killed, and grows within. Simultaneously, Renn has Ludwig face openly the tragedy of the war.

In his book *War and the German Mind*, Pfeiler presents four criteria for excellence in the German war novel: (1) Is the novel truthful? (2) Does the author form his material well? (3) Does he present a vision of his wartime experience? and (4) Can the reader participate finally in the author's rendering of that experience (319)? Remarque's *All Quiet* and the novels discussed in this chapter were all based in authentic combat experience and memory of the Great War, yet the authors' degrees of participation in the war differed widely. The novels of Unruh, Jünger, and Renn clearly "post" the reader within specific battles and combat settings. Remarque, however, avoids that kind of specificity, choosing instead to focus artistically and imaginatively on the tragic personal and generational dimensions of a conflict that led to postwar alienation and estrangement.

It is Remarque who remains conscious of writing a *novel*, not an enlisted man's manual or even a wartime memoir. Unruh and Jünger meet on the common ground of philosophical speculation. Both Unruh and Jünger use the German war experience for loftier dialectical and aesthetic goals, Unruh to free the German national spirit of war altogether, and Jünger to redefine and invigorate the German martial spirit. Renn gives an objective and detailed accounting of his experience on the western front under the guise of an enlisted man, a "mask" he chose for reasons that lay in his family heritage and his rebellion against the vested privilege of the German upper class. In Renn's book, as well as in Remarque's, the intense suffering of the individual in wartime is very clear, though from different perspectives. Remarque creates profound empathy for a victim of military and political connivance and gives new meaning to the phrase "lost generation"—the generation deracinated by fighting in an absurd war.

# Notes and References

## 1. A Citizen of the German Empire

1. For all biographical details on Remarque's ancestry, birth, parents, and life in Osnabrück, I am indebted to the pioneering work of Hanns-Gerd Rabe, "Remarque und Osnabrück: Ein Beitrag zu seiner Biographie" (Remarque and Osnabrück: Contribution to his Biography), *Osnabrücker Mitteilungen* 77 (1970): 196–246, hereafter cited in the text as Rabe, 1970.

2. On the achievements of Weimar culture, see Otto Friedrich, *Before the Deluge* (New York: Harper and Row, 1972). Gay's book (*Weimar Culture: The Outsider as Insider* [New York: Harper and Row, 1968]) is by far the preferred text; it also contains an afterword that summarizes the political wrangling that helped defeat the Weimar government.

3. Erich Maria Remarque, *All Quiet on the Western Front*, trans. A. W. Wheen (1929; reprint, Boston: Little, Brown, 1975), hereafter cited in the text as *AQ*.

4. Especially in the interview by Cyrus Brooks, "Herr Remarque Shuns Literary Honors," *New York Times Magazine*, 22 September 1929, 7, hereafter cited in the text.

5. A recent critique can be found in A. F. Bance, "*Im Westen Nichts Neues*: A Bestseller in Context," *Modern Language Review* 72 (April 1977): 359–73, hereafter cited in the text. Bance never points out that *All Quiet* was a best-selling novel of outstanding merit.

6. Consult relevant sections of Richard Arthur Firda, *Erich Maria Remarque: A Thematic Analysis of His Novels* (New York: Peter Lang, 1988), hereafter cited in the text as Firda, 1988; and Harley U. Taylor, *Erich Maria Remarque: A Literary and Film Biography* (New York: Peter Lang, 1989), hereafter cited in the text.

## 2. The Importance of the Work

1. See Alice P. Hackett and James Henry Burke, *Eighty Years of Best Sellers* (New York: Bowder, 1977), 13.

2. Ernst Jünger, *The Storm of Steel*, trans. Basil Creighton (1929; reprint, New York: Howard Fertig, 1975), hereafter cited in the text as *SS*.

3. Fritz von Unruh, *The Way of Sacrifice*, trans. C. A. Macartney (New York: Alfred A. Knopf, 1928), hereafter cited in the text as *WS*.

## 3. Reception in the Marketplace

1. Ullstein Verlag, *Der Kampf um Remarque* (The Battle around Remarque) (Berlin: Propyläen Verlag, 1929), xeroxed copy in my possession.

2. See Brooks, and Frédéric Lefèvre, "An Hour with Erich Remarque," *Living Age* 339 (December 1930): 344.

3. One of the most reliable accounts of the history of Remarque's submissions of *All Quiet* to German publishers, and its rejections, is found in Peter De Mendelssohn, *S. Fischer und sein Verlag* (Frankfurt: S. Fischer, 1970), 114–17.

4. Details on the firm and its history can be found in Herman Ullstein, *The Rise and Fall of the House of Ullstein* (New York: Simon and Schuster, 1943). *All Quiet* is discussed on pages 148–50.

5. Ernst Toller, "Im Westen Nichts Neues" [review of *Im Westen Nichts Neues*], *Die Literarische Woche* 8 (22 February 1929); Carl Zuckmayer, "Erich Maria Remarque: 'Im Westen Nichts Neues,'" *Berliner Illustrierte* 5 (31 January 1929), reprinted in *Aufruf zum Leben* (Frankfurt: S. Fischer, 1976), 94–97.

6. Firda (1988, 51–52) and Taylor (2) both discuss the background of the controversy surrounding Remarque's purported Jewish ancestry.

7. Mynona [Salomo Friedländer], *Hat Erich Maria Remarque wirklich gelebt?* (Did Remarque Really Live?) (Berlin: Paul Steegemann Verlag, 1929), hereafter cited in the text. Very funny, but also a serious attempt to make sense of a confusing situation, that is, Remarque's and the author's attempts to obfuscate important dates in Remarque's life. Contains a preliminary bibliography of Remarque's writings before his arrival in Berlin.

8. Arnold Zweig, "Kriegsromane" (War Novels), *Die Weltbühne* 25 (April 1929): 598, hereafter cited in the text.

9. See Carl von Ossietzky, "The Remarque Case," trans. John Peet, in *The Stolen Republic: Selected Writings of Carl von Ossietzky*, ed. Bruno Frei (Berlin: Seven Seas Publishers, 1971), 217.

10. Herbert Read, "German War Books," *Manchester Guardian Weekly*, 26 April 1929, 335.

11. Herbert Read, "A Lost Generation" [review of *All Quiet on the Western Front* by Erich Maria Remarque], *The Nation and Athenaeum* 45 (27 April 1929): 116.

12. Ian Hamilton, "The End of War?: A Correspondence between the Author of *All Quiet on the Western Front* and General Sir Ian Hamilton," *Life and Letters* 3 (November 1929), 399, hereafter cited in the text.

13. I am grateful to Little, Brown for their permission in the late 1970s to read correspondence (for research purposes) related to the publication history of *AQ*. This research, including access to some unpublished files, is assimilated into pertinent sections of this chapter.

14. Henry Seidel Canby, "Modern War" [review of *All Quiet on the Western Front* by Erich Maria Remarque], *Saturday Review of Literature* (8 June 1929): 1087, hereafter cited in the text; Frank Hill, "Destroyed by the War" [review of *All Quiet on the Western Front* by Erich Maria Remarque], *New York Herald Tribune*, 2 June 1929.

15. See "Volume Expurgated on Book Club Advice...Toned down for Americans," *New York Times*, 31 May 1929.

16. See "*All Quiet* Arouses German Critics' Ire," *New York Times*, 6 December 1930, for an account of the Nazi picketing.

17. These authors and titles are: Franz Baumer, *E. M. Remarque* (Berlin: Colloquium Verlag, 1976); Christine R. Barker and R. W. Last, *Erich Maria Remarque* (London: Oswald Wolff, 1979); Richard Arthur Firda, *Erich Maria Remarque: A Thematic Analysis of His Novels* (New York: Peter Lang, 1988); Harley V. Taylor, Jr., *Erich Maria Remarque: A Literary and Film Biography* (New York: Peter Lang, 1989); Hans Wagener, *Understanding Erich Maria Remarque* (Columbia: University of South Carolina Press, 1991).

18. Bernard Bergonzi, *Heroes' Twilight: A Study of the Literature of the Great War* (New York: Coward McCann, 1966); Paul Fussell, *The Great War and Modern Memory* (New York: Oxford University Press, 1975).

## 4. A Writer's Apprenticeship

1. Axel Eggebrecht, "Gespräch mit Remarque" (Conversation with Remarque), *Die Literarische Welt*, 14 June 1929; reprinted, in English, in *Boston Evening Transcript*, 21 September 1929.

2. Erich Maria Remarque, *Die Traumbude* (Dream Room) (Dresden: Verlag der Schönheit, 1920, hereafter cited in the text as *DR*. For discussion and analysis, see Richard Arthur Firda, "Young Erich Maria Remarque: *Die Traumbude*," *Monatshefte* 71 (Spring 1979): 49.

3. Axel Eggebrecht, *Der halbe Weg: Zwischenbilanz einer Epoche* (Halfway: Balancing an Epoch) (Reinber: Rowohlt, 1975), 241.

# 6. Aspects of a Literary Style

1. On Remarque's early interest in French paintings, see Curt Riess, *Ascona: Geschichte des seltsamsten Dorfes der Welt* (Zürich: Europa Verlag, 1964), 168–69; and Firda (1988), 83.

# 7. Characters and Characterization

1. My discussion of characterization follows the arguments and presentation in W. J. Harvey, *Character and the Novel* (Ithaca, N.Y.: Cornell University Press, 1965), 30–73, hereafter cited in the text.

2. Forster's famous distinction between "flat" and "rounded" characters is found in *Aspects of the Novel* (New York: Harcourt, Brace, 1954), 103, hereafter cited in the text.

# 8. Adrift: Ending a Trilogy

1. Erich Maria Remarque, *The Road Back*, trans. A. W. Wheen (Boston: Little, Brown: 1931), hereafter cited in the text as *RB*; *Three Comrades*, trans. A. W. Wheen (Boston: Little, Brown: 1937), hereafter cited in the text as *TC*.

2. See especially C. Huntington of Putnam's, unpublished letter to Alfred R. McIntyre of Little, Brown, 14 August 1931, commenting on the "improved" version of *Road*.

3. "Remarque to Flee Spotlight's Glare," *New York Times*, Sunday, 13 October 1929, sec. 3.

4. The "Voss" had already serialized *AQ*. *Pester Lloyd* was read by the large German-speaking community in Hungary's major city; publication there brought Remarque to the attention of Eastern Europeans. *Le Matin* was a prestigious French newspaper; Remarque was well known to its readers.

5. See Arthur Wheen, unpublished letter to Little, Brown, 7 April 1931.

6. These stories—among them, "The Enemy" (29 March 1930) and "Where Karl Had Fought" (23 August 1930)—are distinctly minor efforts. Written during his stint as a popular journalist in Berlin, they have never been collected for publication. The translator is unknown.

7. Clifton Fadiman, "There Is No Road Back," *The Nation* 132 (27 May 1931): 585, hereafter cited in the text.

8. A short account appears in Hanns-Gerd Rabe, "Junglehrer Erich Paul Remark" (Young Teacher Erich Paul Remark), *Merian* (Emsland), no. 24 [undated]: 47–48.

9. "Soldiers' Repartee" [review of *The Road Back*], *Commonweal* (27 May 1931): 89; "Home, Boys, Home" [review of *The Road Back*], *Time*, 21 May 1931; Fadiman, 585.

10. A. W. Smith, "The Man of the Month," [review of *The Road Back*], *Atlantic Monthly* 147 (June 1931): 16.

11. Selected stills were reproduced in *Life*, 28 June 1937, 30, and a negative of the film is housed at the Library of Congress.

12. Otto Biha, "The Road Back of Erich Maria Remarque" [review of *The Road Back*], *Literature of the World Revolution*, no. 5 (1931): 144.

13. The thematic resemblance between *Comrades* and *Farewell to Arms* is noted in J. Donald Adams, "Erich Remarque's New Novel" [review of *Three Comrades*], *New York Times Book Review*, 2 May 1937.

14. See "Funds of Remarque Reported as Seized," *New York Times*, 5 April 1932.

15. Erich Maria Remarque (from Ticino Porto Ronco), unpublished letter (in German) to Alfred R. McIntyre, Little, Brown, 27 January 1936; copy in my possession.

16. Further information on the tangled relationship between Jutta Ilse Zambona and Remarque can be found in Taylor, 56–57.

17. Bernard DeVoto, "Germany in the Vortex," [review of *Three Comrades*], *Saturday Review of Literature* (1 May 1937): 3.

18. F. C. Weiskopf, "Roman im Niemandsland" (A Novel from Nowhere), in *Literarische Streifzüge* (Berlin: Aufbau Verlag, 1956), 55–58, hereafter cited in the text.

## 9. Déjà Vu: Exile and After

1. Charles Poore, "Blackout before the Deluge" [review of *Arch of Triumph*], *New York Times Book Review*, 20 January 1946, 1.

2. Axel Silenius, "Die Schicksalslinie eines Emigranten" (The Fateful Pattern of an Emigrant), *Tribüne: Zeitschrift zum Verständnis des Judenproblems* 71, no. 27 (1968): 2914. For a similar analysis, see Werner Suhr, "Der Fall Remarque" (Remarque's Case), *Neues Europa: Deutsche Stimme* 2, no. 13 (1947): 25.

3. Erich Maria Remarque, *A Time to Love and a Time to Die* (New York: Harcourt, Brace, 1954), published in German as *Zeit zu lebers und Zeit zu sterben*.

4. Hans Habe, *Erfahrungen* (Experiences) (Olten: Walter Verlag, 1973), 142. Habe calls Remarque the "last citizen of Weimar" and, in the same essay, claims that Remarque resented having a greater reputation outside of Germany than in his homeland (141).

## 10. Film Classic: The Film Adaptation of *All Quiet on the Western Front*

1. I have relied on the following accounts for my discussion of the feature film of *All Quiet on the Western Front* (hereafter cited in the text as *Front*): Bosley Crowther, *The Great Films: Fifty Golden Years of Motion*

*Pictures* (New York: G. P. Putnam's Sons, 1967), 77; John Cutts, "All Quiet on the Western Front," *Films and Filming* 9 (April 1963): 55; Stanley Hochman, ed., *American Film Directors* (New York: Frederich Ungar, 1974), 323; Dorothy B. Jones, "War without Glory," *Quarterly of Film, Radio, and Television* 8 (Spring 1954): 273; Jay Leyda, ed., *Voices of Film Experience* (New York: Macmillan, 1977), 312; Basil Wright, *The Long View* (New York: Alfred A. Knopf, 1974), 164; all hereafter cited in the text.

2. See Matthew J. Bruccoli, ed,. *F. Scott Fitzgerald's Screenplay for "Three Comrades" by Erich Maria Remarque* (Carbondale and Edwardsville: Southern Illinois University Press, 1978). This published screenplay is not the final version used in the film.

3. See John Drinkwater, *The Life and Adventures of Carl Laemmle* (New York: G. P. Putnam's Sons, 1931), 227.

4. Ivan Butler, *The War Film* (Cranbury, N.J.: A. S. Barnes, 1974), 12.

5. "Confers on New War Film," *New York Times*, 11 August 1929.

6. John McCarten, "Still Lively" [film review of *All Quiet on the Western Front*], *New Yorker* 26 (5 August 1950): 37.

7. Copy of (unpublished) continuity and subtitles for *Front* in my possession; obtained from New York State Archives, Albany, New York. In the central portions of my analysis I rely on the copies of the stills and continuity found in *Der Film Im Westen Nichts Neues in Bildern* (Stills from *All Quiet on the Western Front*) (Berlin: Ernst Rowohlt Verlag, 1931). This text reproduces most of the stills from the film and is housed at the Library of Congress. A commercial videotape version of *Front* is also available in the United States.

8. Andrew Sarris, *The American Cinema: Directors, 1929–1968* (New York: E. P. Dutton, 1968), 119.

9. "*All Quiet* Arouses German Critics' Ire," *New York Times*, 6 December 1930.

10. Carl von Ossietzky, "Remarque-Film," *Die Weltbühne* 26 (16 December 1930): 889.

11. Albert C. Grzesinski, *Inside Germany*, trans. Alexander S. Lipshitz (New York: Dutton, 1939), 134.

12. Walther Victor, "Im Westen Nichts Neues," in *Köpfe und Herzen* (Heads and Hearts) (Weimar: Thuringer Volksverlag, 1949), 206.

## 11. Evaluation: *All Quiet on the Western Front* and Other German War Novels

1. A standard and recommended discussion is William K. Pfeiler, *War and the German Mind* (New York: Columbia University Press, 1941), 3–37, 140, hereafter cited in the text.

2. Ludwig Renn, *War*, trans. Willa and Edwin Muir (New York: Dodd, Mead, 1929; reprint, New York: Howard Fertig, 1988), hereafter cited in the text as *W*.

3. Ludwig Harig, "Verdun ist keine Taube" (Verdun is Nothing Easy), in *Romane von gestern, heute gelesen* (Novels of yesterday, read today), vol. 2, ed. Marcel Reich-Ranicki (Frankfurt: S. Fischer, 1989), 16.

4. Recommended for understanding the background of *Steel* is Gerhard Loose, *Ernst Jünger* (New York: Twayne, 1974), especially chs. 1–2.

5. This essay is pivotal to understanding Jünger's position on the "necessity" of war—so totally different and ideologically distanced from Remarque—and can be found in Ernst Jünger, *Essays I: Betrachtungen zur Zeit*, vol. 5 of *Werke* (Stuttgart: Ernst Klett Verlag, 1960), 13–108.

6. Alfred Antkowiak discusses Renn in the context of leftist ideology in "Ludwig Renn," in *Ludwig Renn: Erich Maria Remarque: Leben und Werk* (Ludwig Renn: Erich Maria Remarque: Life and Work) (Berlin: Volk und Wissen/Volkseigener Verlag, 1965), 1.

7. Ludwig Renn, "Nachwort" ("Afterword"), in *Krieg: Nachkrieg* (War: The Aftermath of War), vol. 3 of *Gesammelte Werke in Einzelausgaben* (Collected Works In Individual Editions) (Berlin: Aufbau Verlag, 1964), 519, hereafter cited in the text.

# Selected Bibliography

## Primary Works

*All Quiet on the Western Front*. Translated by A. W. Wheen. Boston: Little, Brown, 1929; reprint, Boston: Little, Brown, 1975. Originally published in German as *Im Westen Nichts Neues* (Berlin: Propläen Verlag, 1929).

*The Road Back*. Translated by A. W. Wheen. Boston: Little, Brown, 1931. Originally published as *Der Weg zurück* (Berlin: Propyläen Verlag, 1931).

*Three Comrades*. Translated by A. W. Wheen. Boston: Little, Brown, 1937. Originally published in German as *Drei Kameraden* (Amsterdam: Querido Verlag, 1938).

*A Time to Love and a Time to Die*. New York: Harcourt, Brace, 1954. Originally published in German as *Zeit zu leben und Zeit zu sterben* (Cologne: Kiepenheuer and Witsch, 1954).

*Die Traumbude* (Dream Room) (Dresden: Verlag der Schönheit, 1920).

## Secondary Works

### Books

Barker, Christine R., and R. W. Last. *Erich Maria Remarque*. London: Oswald Wolff, 1979. Slim, overall assessment of the novels. One of the first books published during the current revival of interest in Remarque.

Baumer, Franz. *E. M. Remarque* (in German). Berlin: Colloquium Verlag, 1976. Less to offer than Barker and Last, with minimal discussion of texts.

Bergonzi, Bernard. *Heroes' Twilight: A Study of the Literature of the Great War*. New York: Coward McCann, 1966. Standard discussion of mostly English-language fiction about the Great War. Good introduction to the subject, however.

Butler, Ivan. *The War Film*. Cranbury, N.J.: A. S. Barnes, 1974. Good overall discussion of how war is handled by film directors in the genre of war films. Covers the feature film version of *All Quiet*.

Eggebrecht, Axel. *Der halbe Weg: Zwischenbilanz einer Epoche* (in German). Reinber: Rowohlt, 1975. Interesting accounts of Remarque's Berlin days working in journalism by an observer of the time.

Firda, Richard Arthur. *Erich Maria Remarque: A Thematic Analysis of His Novels*. New York: Peter Lang, 1988. Biography and a discussion of the novels.

Friedrich, Otto. *Before the Deluge*. New York: Harper and Row, 1972. Standard account of German Weimar culture and its representative figures.

Fussell, Paul. *The Great War and Modern Memory*. New York: Oxford University Press, 1975. Discussion of classic English and European novels of World War I. Thematic arrangement.

Gay, Peter. *Weimar Culture: The Outsider as Insider*. New York: Harper and Row, 1968. Essays on the artists, politicians, and culture of the period. Clearly written standard text by an academician.

Habe, Hans. *Erfahrungen* (in German). Olten: Walter Verlag, 1973. Contains a perceptive essay on Remarque's status as a writer among his German contemporaries.

Jünger, Ernst. *Essays I: Betrachtungen zur Zeit*. Vol. 5 of *Werke* (in German). Stuttgart: Ernst Klett Verlag, 1960. Opinions and thoughts on war's aesthetic and heroic aspects by a contemporary (and rival) of Remarque.

———. *The Storm of Steel*. Translated by Basil Creighton. London: Chatto & Windus, 1929; reprint, New York: Howard Fertig, 1975. Originally published in German as *In Stahlgewittern* (1919).

Kamla, Thomas A. *Confrontation with Exile: Studies in the German Novel*. Bern: Herbert Lang, 1975. Pioneering English-language study of the exile experience in the works of German writers, including Remarque.

Loose, Gerhard. *Ernst Jünger*. New York: Twayne, 1974. Study of Jünger's works, including extensive analysis of *The Storm of Steel*.

Mynona [Salomo Friedländer]. *Hat Erich Maria Remarque wirklich gelebt?* (in German). Berlin: Paul Steegemann Verlag, 1929. Famous satire on Remarque. Includes bibliography.

Pfeiler, William K. *War and the German Mind*. New York: Columbia University Press, 1941. Discussion of German World War I novels.

Renn, Ludwig. *War*. Translated by Willa and Edwin Muir. New York: Dodd, Mead, 1929; reprint, New York: Howard Fertig, 1988. Originally published as *Krieg* (1928).

Taylor, Harley U. *Erich Maria Remarque: A Literary and Film Biography*. New York: Peter Lang, 1989. A recent attempt to integrate biography and cinema in the author's career. A point of departure.

Ullstein Verlag. *Der Kampf um Remarque* (in German). Berlin: Propyläen Verlag, 1929. Publicity brochure by Remarque's German publisher for the sale and promotion of *All Quiet*.

Unruh, Fritz von. *The Way of Sacrifice*. Translated by C. A. Macartney. New York: Alfred A. Knopf, 1928. Originally published in German as *Der Opfergang* (1919). Needs to be updated.

Wagener, Hans. *Understanding Erich Maria Remarque*. Columbia, S.C.: University of South Carolina Press, 1991. Handbook. Introduction to the novels.

Weiskopf, F. C. *Literarische Streifzüge* (in German). Berlin: Aufbau Verlag, 1956. Criticism of *Three Comrades* and the issue of popular literature.

Zuckmayer, Carl. *Aufruf zum Leben: Porträts und Zeugnise aux bewegten Zeiten* (in German). Frankfurt: S. Fischer, 1976. On page 93 appears a remembrance of how Zuckmayer, a leading prose writer of the Weimar period and a contemporary of Remarque, came to write one of the first laudatory reviews of *All Quiet*.

## Articles and Parts of Books

Antkowiak, Alfred. "Erich Maria Remarque" (in German). In *Ludwig Renn: Erich Maria Remarque: Leben und Werk*. Berlin: Volk and Wissen/ Volkseigener Verlag, 1965. Remarque's novels seen from a contemporary Marxist point of view. Fair but slanted.

Bance, A. F. "*Im Westen Nichts Neues*: A Bestseller in Context." *Modern Language Review* 72 (April 1977): 359–73. The best-seller strategy behind the marketing of Remarque's novel. Critical of the author.

Biha, Otto. "The Road Back of Erich Remarque" [review of *The Road Back* by Erich Maria Remarque]. *Literature of the World Revolution*, no. 5 (1931): 144–48. Review and extensive critique of *Road* by a prominent European leftist. Important for its topicality.

Brooks, Cyrus. "Herr Remarque Shuns Literary Honors." *New York Times Magazine*, 22 September 1929. Interview with Remarque in Berlin on the writing of *All Quiet*.

Duesberg, W. "Telephoning Remarque." *Living Age* 340 (June 1931): 372–75. Originally published in Spanish in *Gazeta Literaria* (Madrid). Interview with Remarque in Berlin before the publication of *Road* and after *All Quiet* was published. Provides clues to his writing process for an American audience.

Emmel, Hildegard. "The Novel during the Weimar Republic." In *History of the German Novel*. Detroit: Wayne State University Press, 1984. Succinct coverage of *All Quiet* and other contemporary German war novels. More than one-line references of the genre.

Firda, Richard Arthur. "Young Erich Maria Remarque: *Die Traumbude.*" *Monatshefte* 71 (Spring 1979): 49–51. Remarque's artist novel and its theme, characters, and autobiographical references.

Hagbolt, Peter. "Ethical and Social Problems in the German War Novel." *Journal of English and Germanic Philology* 32 (January 1933): 21–32. Academic thematic commentary on a host of German war novels. Remarque's *All Quiet* is discussed in a philosophical context.

Hamilton, Ian. "The End of War? A Correspondence between the Author of *All Quiet on the Western Front* and General Sir Ian Hamilton." *Life and Letters* 3 (November 1929): 399–411. Extracts from an exchange of letters between Remarque and a general in the British army during the Great War.

Harig, Ludwig. "Verdun ist keine Taube" (in German). In *Romane von gestern, heute gelesen*, vol. 2, edited by Marcel Reich-Ranicki. Frankfurt: S. Fischer, 1989. Discusses Unruh's novel *Der Opfergang* (The Way of Sacrifice) for a contemporary reader.

Jones, Dorothy B. "War without Glory." *Quarterly of Film, Radio, and Television* 8 (Spring 1954): 273–89. Important and lengthy analysis of feature film adaptation of *All Quiet*.

Lefèvre, Frédéric. "An Hour with Erich Remarque." *Living Age* 339 (December 1930): 344–49. Originally published in French in *Nouvelles Littéraires*. Described as "the first account ever published of a conversation with Erich Remarque." Important for its original appearance in a respected literary journal.

Milch, W. J. "The Development of Ernst Jünger." *The Nineteenth Century and After* 139 (January 1946): 35–39. Discusses Jünger's political and philosophical attitudes toward soldiering. Presents Jünger as a defender of war.

Ossietzky, Carl von. "Remarque-Film" (in German). *Die Weltbühne* 26 (December 1930): 889–91. A liberal, leftist critique of the Weimar government's decision to ban the showing of the film adaptation of *All Quiet*.

———. "The Remarque Case." Translated by John Peet. In *The Stolen Republic: Selected Writings of Carl von Ossietzky*, edited by Bruno Frei.

Berlin: Seven Seas Publishers, 1971. Remarque as seen by German leftists in 1932.

Rabe, Hanns-Gerd. "Remarque und Osnabrück: Ein Beitrag zu seiner Biographie" (in German). *Osnabrücker Mitteilungen* 77 (1970): 196–246. Essential basic account of Remarque's ties to his birthplace, his family and ancestry, and background to *All Quiet* and his other novels. Written by a contemporary and friend of Remarque.

Renn, Ludwig. "Nachwort" (in German). In *Krieg: Nachkrieg*, vol. 3 of *Gessammelte Werke in Einzelausgaben*. Berlin: Aufbau Verlag, 1964. The author gives background on *War*.

Sclutius, Karl Hugo. "Pazifistische Kriegspropaganda" (in German). *Die Weltbühne* 25 (April 1929): 517–22. Essay-review of *All Quiet* and Renn's *War*.

Zweig, Arnold. "Kriegsromane" (in German). *Die Weltbühne* 25 (April 1929): 597–99. Follow-up and critical response to Sclutius article. Remarque's failure to write a novel attacking German capitalists was a disappointment to Zweig, himself the writer of a popular Weimar war novel.

# Index

# The Author

Richard Arthur Firda is an associate professor of German at Georgia State University in Atlanta, where he teaches courses in the German language and in contemporary German literature. He holds degrees from George Washington University and Harvard University, where he received his M.A. and Ph.D. in comparative literature. He has written on topics from Erich Maria Remarque and Peter Handke to German film. In 1991 he published a work on Peter Handke in the World Authors Series for Twayne Publishers. At present he is engaged in a study of the German adventure novelist Karl May.

# Twayne's World Authors Series

These recently published Twayne titles are available by mail. To order directly, return the coupon below to: Twayne Publishers, Att: LP, 866 Third Avenue, New York, N.Y. 10022, or call toll-free 1-800-323-7445 (9:00 A.M. to 9:00 P.M. EST).

| Line | Quantity | ISBN | Author/Title | Price |
|------|----------|------|--------------|-------|
| 1 | _____ | 0805782907 | Barbour/MICHAEL ONDAATJE | $22.95 |
| 2 | _____ | 0805782982 | Schuster/MARGUERITE DURAS | $22.95 |
| 3 | _____ | 0805782826 | Kelly/MEDIEVAL FRENCH ROMANCE | $24.95 |
| 4 | _____ | 0805782737 | Conroy/MONTESQUIEU REVISITED | $22.95 |
| 5 | _____ | 0805782745 | Bucknall/MARCEL PROUST REVISITED | $24.95 |
| 6 | _____ | 0805782885 | Talbot/STENDHAL REVISITED | $22.95 |
| 7 | _____ | 0805782761 | Falk/ELIAS CANETTI | $22.95 |
| 8 | _____ | 0805782893 | Tittler/MANUEL PUIG | $22.95 |
| 9 | _____ | 0805782796 | Wright/WOLE SOYINKA REVISITED | $22.95 |
| 10 | _____ | 0805782818 | Firda/PETER HANDKE | $22.95 |
| 11 | _____ | 0805782680 | Vickery/ALEXANDER PUSHKIN, REVISED EDITION | $22.95 |
| 12 | _____ | 0805764240 | Alexander/ISAAC BASHEVIS SINGER | $22.95 |

Sub-total _____

Please add postage and handling costs—$2.00 for the first book and 75¢ for each additional book _____

Sales tax—if applicable _____

TOTAL _____

| | | Lines | Units |
|--|--|-------|-------|

Control No. [          ]    Ord. Type [ SPCA ] [    |    ]

___ Enclosed is my check/money order payble to Macmillan Publishing Company.

___ Bill my ☐AMEX ☐MasterCard ☐Visa ☐Discover    Exp. date _____

Card # _____ Signature _____

*Charge orders valid only with signature*

Ship to: _____

_____

_____ Zip Code

For charge orders only:

Bill to: _____

_____

_____ Zip Code

For information regarding bulk purchases, please write to Managing Editor at the above address. Publisher's prices are subject to change without notice. Allow 4–6 weeks for delivery.                    Promo # 78728 FC2615

## Twayne's Critical Essays Series on World Literature

These recently published Twayne titles are available by mail. To order directly, return the coupon below to: Twayne Publishers, Att: LP, 866 Third Avenue, New York, N.Y. 10022, or call toll-free 1-800-323-7445 (9:00 A.M. to 9:00 P.M. EST).

| Line | Quantity | ISBN | Author/Title | Price |
|------|----------|------|--------------|-------|
| 1 | _____ | 0816188408 | McCombs, ed./ MARGARET ATWOOD | $42.00 |
| 2 | _____ | 0816188459 | Kanes, ed./ HONORE DE BALZAC | $42.00 |
| 3 | _____ | 0816188386 | Knapp, ed./ ALBERT CAMUS | $42.00 |
| 4 | _____ | 0816188254 | El Saffar, ed./ CERVANTES | $42.00 |
| 5 | _____ | 0816188432 | Eekamn, ed./ ANTON CHEKHOV | $42.00 |
| 6 | _____ | 0816188491 | Mazzotta, ed./ DANTE | $42.00 |
| 7 | _____ | 0816188327 | Atchity, et al, eds./ HOMER | $42.00 |
| 8 | _____ | 0816188483 | Gross, ed./ FRANZ KAFKA | $42.00 |
| 9 | _____ | 0816188378 | Ezergailis, ed./ THOMAS MANN | $42.00 |
| 10 | _____ | 0816188343 | McMurray, ed./ GABRIEL GARCIA MARQUEZ | $42.00 |
| 11 | _____ | 0816188335 | Bucknall, ed./ MARCEL PROUST | $42.00 |
| 12 | _____ | 0816188394 | Wilcocks, ed./ JEAN-PAUL SARTRE | $42.00 |

Sub-total _____

Please add postage and handling costs—$2.00 for the first book and 75¢ for each additional book _____

Sales tax—if applicable _____

TOTAL _____

Lines  Units

Control No. [          ]  Ord. Type [ SPCA ]  [       ]

__ Enclosed is my check/money order payble to Macmillan Publishing Company.

__ Bill my  ☐ AMEX ☐ MasterCard ☐ Visa ☐ Discover    Exp. date _____

Card # _____ Signature _____

*Charge orders valid only with signature*

Ship to: _____

_____

_____ Zip Code

For charge orders only:

Bill to: _____

_____

_____ Zip Code

For information regarding bulk purchases, please write to Managing Editor at the above address. Publisher's prices are subject to change without notice. Allow 4–6 weeks for delivery.

Promo # 78722 FC2609